The

Roots:

Our Legacy in the History of the
Modern Church

Dr. Robert E. Johnson Sr., DRE

The Roots:

Our Legacy In The History of the Modern Church

Copyright © ELOHIM MULTIMEDIA
Elohim Multimedia 2013
ISBN 987-1-304-69816-2
All Rights Reserved

𝔉𝔒ℜ𝔚𝔄ℜ𝔇

Dr. Robert Johnson's love for history and church history in particular will be very evident as you study this [work]. Studying Church History with Bishop Robert Johnson at the helm will cause you to feel as if you are an eye witness to the events as they unfold.

I hope this [work] leaves you with a love for history and Church History in particular and as you delve into its study, you will find God's word is full of prophetic truths that are revealed in the history of the Church.

Dr. Robert Johnson is a historian extraordinaire. We hope you enjoy this [book] and his extensive compilation of material as we have enjoyed it [as well]..

Dr. Ann T. Newell, Assistant President
Christian Outreach Bible Institute
Fayetteville, North Carolina

Dr. Robert Johnson's course titled Church History is an exciting course where you will discover the Foundation of the church and the History of the Church during the Apostolic Age. Dr. Robert Johnson is a prolific professor, preacher and student of God's word.

This [book] will help you understand the major divisions of church history and the key events within each division. You will gain insight and an overview of the various doctrines within the general periods of the church.

I hope this study in Church History will help you gain a fuller knowledge about the history of the church and the truth of God's Word.

Dr. Joanie T. Greene, President
Christian Outreach Bible Institute
Fayetteville, North Carolina

ACKNOWLEDGEMENT

This work has been a long time coming and there are just so many people to thank for helping me get this far. However, I want to point out the most influential persons that gave me the backing and support to get it done.

First and foremost, I appreciate and thank the person that I call "my prime rib" and that is my wife of over 44 years, Jacqueline Faye Saunders Johnson. She has been the one to support and push all of my endeavors in life and I would not be the person that I am without her support.

Then the two people that believed in me and became my mentors both spiritually and educationally, Chief Apostle Monroe R. Saunders, Sr. who has departed and Mother Alberta B. Saunders, who has become my mother since my own dear mother has also departed. A whole section of this work is dedicated to the Chief Apostle because he was my greatest influence and role model.

I thank also my own dear parents, John E. and Desiree Johnson, who have departed. They were the ones who brought me into this world and pushed me to go to school and study and get the education that they did not have the opportunity to get.

I thank Dr. Ann Newell and Dr. Joanie Greene who pushed me to finish my doctoral work and produce this book that you now hold in your hands. I appreciate the students that sat under my teaching over the years and even helped to bring it all together in a form that all could read. One outstanding student that I had and acknowledge is Dr.

Gregory Robinson who created one of the charts that you find in this book, Then I want to thank the Pastors of the 2nd Episcopal Diocese especially Elder Albert Thompson who videoed my teachings and gave insight to bring it all together. For this I will be eternally grateful for their years of support.

I also thank my three children, Keturah, Katherine and Robert, Jr. who have been an inspiration to me as well to exceed and do what has been my God-given talent and I appreciate them so very much.

Finally, I thank Briana CaBell and Elohim Multimedia for taking the time to get all of my notes and putting it together in a format that would produce the book that you now hold. I do hope that you get insight into our history and are blessed by what you read and expand your knowledge and use for the furtherance of your personal knowledge and ministry.

Your servant,

Dr. Robert E. Johnson, Sr.

"God damn America!" In the fall of 2008, newspapers, talk shows and internet blogs exploded with news that the Rev. Jeremiah Wright had denounced the United States with inflammatory language. The African American minister from Chicago's Trinity Church, Wright's most famous parishioner was the leading Democratic contender for the presidential nomination, Barack Obama. The temple where Obama had found religion The sanctuary where he was married. The "holy" pool where his daughters had been baptized. Rev. Wright, a former Marine with a Ph.D., had served as his spiritual mentor.

While many white voters were surprised, puzzled, shocked and angered by Wright's angry rhetoric, African Americans were less so. The unique African American experience makes us much more tolerant and understanding of such extreme attitudes by our own. Obama seized the moment to deliver a profound meditation on race in America, a speech titled "A More Perfect Union." Tracing the deep historical roots of racial inequality and injustice, Obama put Wright's anger into historical context. In very personal terms, he also described his experience at Trinity:

Like most other black churches, Trinity's services are full of the spirit of laughter and humor. There is dancing and singing, screaming and shouting, running and jumping and even strange other-worldly languages that may seem odd or even frightening to an outsiders ear. The Black church contains the kindness and cruelty, the fierce intelligence and the shocking ignorance, the struggles and successes, the love and yes, the bitterness and bias that make up the Black experience in America.

Eventually Obama broke ties with Wright and left Trinity for what are considered political and personal reasons, but his speech illuminated the role of the Black church in the African American experience. It afforded the nation a renewed interest, and for some, a new interest in the inner-workings of the African American church. As historian

Anthea Butler has observed, the church has been profoundly shaped by regional differences, North and South, East and West, yet in both the private and public spheres, the church was, and remains, sustained and animated by idea of freedom.

The term "the Black church" evolved from the phrase "the Negro church," the title of a pioneering sociological study of African American Protestant churches at the turn of the century by W.E.B. Du Bois. In its origins, the phrase was largely an academic category. Many African Americans did not necessarily think of themselves as belonging to "the Negro church," but rather described themselves according to denominational affiliations such as Methodist, Baptist, Presbyterian, and even "Saint" of the Sanctified tradition. African American Christians were never monolithic; they have always been diverse and their churches highly decentralized.

Today "the Black church" is widely understood to include the following ten major Black Protestant denominations: the National Baptist Convention, the National Baptist Convention of America, the Progressive National Convention, Pentecostal Assemblies of the World, Full Gospel Baptist, the United Churches of Jesus Christ, the African Methodist Episcopal Church, the African Methodist Episcopal Zion Church, the Christian Methodist Episcopal Church and the Church of God in Christ.

In light of the recent interest in the Black church there is no better time to look into our history. Throughout this book you will find several questions in each section. As you read through this work as well as the Bible, I urge you to take the time to answer these questions as I believe they will be of great benefit to your understanding of the theme. Let us now take a look back not only into our current church but also at the foundation of the church itself.

TIMELINE OF CHURCH HISTORY

inspired by a timeline from Conciliar Press

Part 1

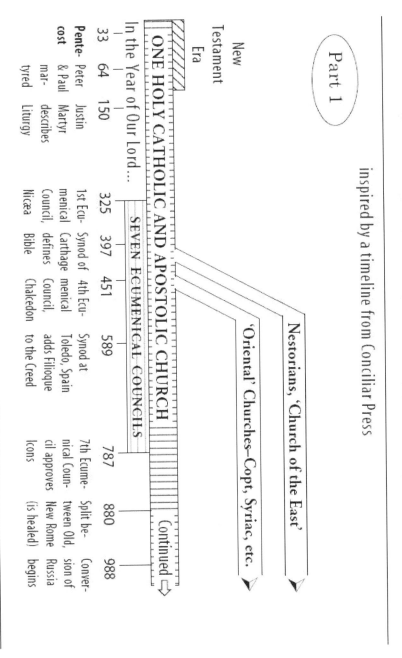

New Testament Era

ONE HOLY CATHOLIC AND APOSTOLIC CHURCH

In the Year of Our Lord...

SEVEN ECUMENICAL COUNCILS

Nestorians, 'Church of the East'

'Oriental' Churches—Copt, Syriac, etc.

Continued ⇒

	Pentecost
33	Peter & Paul martyred
64	Justin Martyr describes Liturgy
150	1st Ecumenical Council, Nicæa
325	Synod of Carthage defines Bible
397	4th Ecumenical Council, Chalcedon
451	Synod at Toledo, Spain adds Filioque to the Creed
589	7th Ecumenical Council approves Icons
787	Split between Old, New Rome (is healed)
880	Conversion of Russia begins
988	

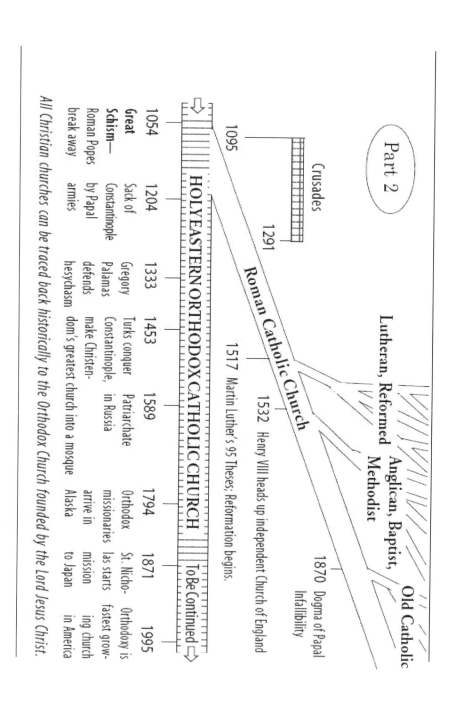

Part 2

Crusades
1095 — 1291

Roman Catholic Church

Lutheran, Reformed   Anglican, Baptist,   Old Catholic
Methodist

1517 Martin Luther's 95 Theses; Reformation begins.

1532 Henry VIII heads up independent Church of England

1870 Dogma of Papal Infallibility

HOLY EASTERN ORTHODOX CATHOLIC CHURCH   To Be Continued

1054	1204	1333	1453	1589	1794	1871	1995
Great Schism— Roman Popes break away	Sack of Constantinople by Papal armies	Gregory Palamas defends hesychasm	Turks conquer Constantinople, dom's greatest church into a mosque	Patriarchate in Russia	Orthodox missionaries arrive in mission	St. Nicho- las starts fastest grow- ing church to Japan	Orthodoxy is fastest grow- ing church in America

All Christian churches can be traced back historically to the Orthodox Church founded by the Lord Jesus Christ.

Part 1

𝔒𝔲𝔯 𝔆𝔥𝔲𝔯𝔠𝔥 𝔦𝔫 𝔥𝔦𝔰𝔱𝔬𝔯𝔭

1. **The Day of Pentecost:** Luke 24:40, Acts 1:4; Acts 2:1-4; 2:38 – Gospel of John passion **Aim:** To establish a scriptural basis for the Pentecostal experience.

2. **Speaking in Tongues (Glossolalia):** Sign and Gift. Acts 2:4; 10:44-46; 19:1-6' and I Cor. 12-14. **Aim:** To understand the distinction which Pentecostals make between "tongues" as a sign and tongues as a gift of the Spirit.

3. **Doctrinal Presupposition.** A summary of Pentecostal belief in relation to other "Bible believing" groups. **Aim:** To understand how and why Pentecostals tend to be evangelical and fundamental in their "theology".

4. **Doctrinal Differences**. (The Godhead) Matt. 28:19; Acts 2:38. **Aim**: To understand the differences Pentecostals make between the "Oneless" groups and the Trinitarian groups.

5. **View of Jesus among some Early Church Fathers.** Leading to the formulation of the Doctrine of the Trinity. Justin Martyr (103-166 A.D.) **Aim**: To seek to understand why and how Jesus was conceived of as "a second God".

6. **Irenaeus (c202 A.D).** Jesus, the incarnation of Logos' representative man.
   Aim: To seek to understand the origin of certain thoughts and factors leading to a doctrinal statement of the relation of Father, Son, and Holy Spirit (the Trinity).

7. **The Monarchians:** Jesus, Son of God by Adoption.
   Aim: To seek to understand the problem faced when one seeks to fit Jesus in thought patterns of any age.

8. **Tertullian (160 to 220 AD).** Jesus, both God and Man.
   Aim: To seek to understand the meaning of "person", "substance", "subordination", and "Christ", as used by Tertullian with reference to Jesus, the Son' in relation to God, the Father.

9. **Clement of Alexandria (215 AD). Christian Gnosticism –** Logos, teacher of all men, became incarnate in Jesus, but Jesus only seemed to have a human body.
   Aim: To seek to understand how this strand of thought was to affect the formulation of the Doctrine of the Trinity and how it relates to later Christian thought.

10. **Origen (185 to 254 AD):** God, Creator – Jesus Christ, the God-man—co-equal, co-eternal, subordinate, the Holy Spirit, un-created.
    Aim: To seek to understand Origen's teaching of the Godhead—how men derive their existence form the Father, their rational nature from the Son, and their Sanctification from the Spirit.

11. **The Arian Controversy.** Two strands of thought: (1) God is eternal, the Son is eternal, the Son is the "unbegotten begotten" (2) The Sod has a beginning, God is without beginning, the Son is not a part of God.
Aim: To seek to understand the dynamics of these two strains and how a conflict was inevitable.

12. **Constantine the Great.** Mediator of the Dispute.
Aim: To seek an understanding of the motives and methods involved in the Emperor's attempt to settle the controversy.

13. **The Council of Nicea (325 AD):** The Nicean Creed.
Aim: To seek to understand what framers sought to do in the Creed and what were some immediate and long range results.

14. **Spiritual Gifts from the Fourth Century Onward.** A general assumption. The re-assertion of the Charismatic dynamic.
Aim: To understand the historic assumption held with regards to supernatural gifts after the third century and the circumstances or situations out of which the charismatic dynamic arose.

15. **The Church Organizes and Centralizes.** The Canon and Hierarchy.
Aim: To understand the special problems faced by the Church which brought on the need for a collection of an agreed upon document (Canon of Scripture), an administrative hierarchy, and the consequences for deviating points of view.

16. **Montanism.** A Charismatic Beginning.

Aim: To understand what Montanus believed and taught about the gifts of the Spirit and the coming of Christ's kingdom, and the authority of the Church.

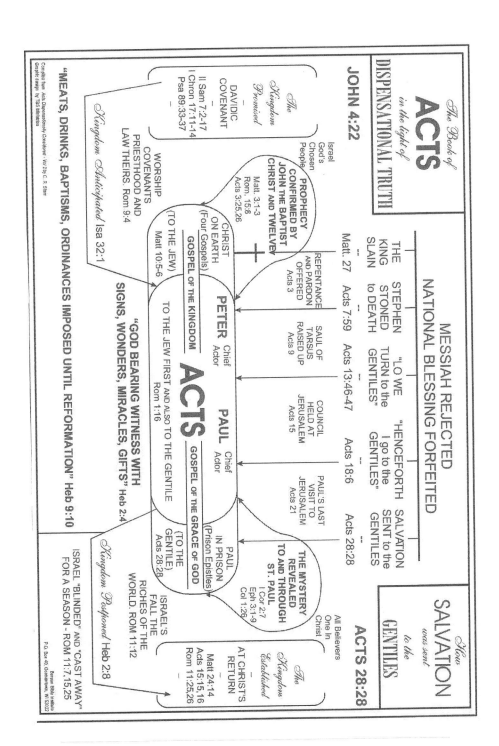

The Book of
ACTS
in the light of
DISPENSATIONAL TRUTH

Compiled from: Acts Dispensationally Considered - Vol 2 by C. R. Stam
Graphic design by TBS Ministries

JOHN 4:22

The Kingdom Promised

Israel
God's
Chosen
People

DAVIDIC COVENANT
II Sam 7:2-17
I Chron 17:11-14
Psa 89:33-37

Kingdom Anticipated Isa 32:1

WORSHIP
COVENANTS
PRIESTHOOD AND
LAW THEIRS. Rom 9:4

PROPHECY
CONFIRMED BY
JOHN THE BAPTIST
CHRIST AND TWELVE
Matt. 3:1-3
Rom. 15:8
Acts 3:25,26

CHRIST
ON EARTH
(Four Gospels)

GOSPEL OF THE KINGDOM
(TO THE JEW)
Matt 10:5-6

MESSIAH REJECTED
NATIONAL BLESSING FORFEITED

THE
KING
SLAIN
Matt. 27

STEPHEN
STONED
to DEATH
Acts 7:59

"LO WE
TURN to the
GENTILES"
Acts 13:46-47

"HENCEFORTH
I go to the
GENTILES"
Acts 18:6

SALVATION
SENT to the
GENTILES
Acts 28:28

REPENTANCE
AND PARDON
OFFERED
Acts 3

SAUL OF
TARSUS
RAISED UP
Acts 9

COUNCIL
HELD AT
JERUSALEM
Acts 15

PAUL'S LAST
VISIT TO
JERUSALEM
Acts 21

PETER Chief Actor

ACTS

PAUL Chief Actor

GOSPEL OF THE GRACE OF GOD
(TO THE GENTILE)
Acts 28:28

TO THE JEW FIRST AND ALSO TO THE GENTILE
Rom 1:16

PAUL
IN PRISON
(Prison Epistles)

THE MYSTERY
REVEALED
TO AND THROUGH
ST. PAUL
I Cor 2:7
Eph 3:1-9
Col 1:26

Now **SALVATION** *was sent* to the **GENTILES**

ACTS 28:28

All Believers
One In
Christ

ISRAEL'S
FALL THE
RICHES OF THE
WORLD. ROM 11:12

The Kingdom Established

Matt 24:14
AT CHRIST'S
RETURN
Acts 15:15,16
Rom 11:25,26

Kingdom Postponed Heb 2:8

ISRAEL "BLINDED" AND "CAST AWAY"
FOR A SEASON - ROM 11:7,15,25

"GOD BEARING WITNESS WITH
SIGNS, WONDERS, MIRACLES, GIFTS" Heb 2:4

"MEATS, DRINKS, BAPTISMS, ORDINANCES IMPOSED UNTIL REFORMATION" Heb 9:10

Berean Bible Institute
P.O. Box 40, Germantown, WI 53022

The Book of Acts

Acts is actually a continuation of Luke's Gospel. Luke connects the two books by introducing Acts with these words, "The former treatise have I made O Theophilus, of all that Jesus began both to do and teach "(1:1). The former treatise refers to the Gospel of Luke, in which Luke told the story of what Jesus began to do and teach while He was on earth. Acts begins where Luke left off, by recording what Jesus continued to do by the power of the Holy Spirit working through the church.

What is the heading of the Book of Acts in your Bible? Some read "The Acts" while the traditional heading is "The Acts of the Apostles". However, this book is not really a record of the Acts of the Apostles. Instead, it records the **acts of the Holy Spirit** working through the church. The apostles are scarcely mentioned, with the exception of Peter and Paul. Yet, the Holy Spirit is mentioned about 70 times. Other people, such as Philip, Stephen, Barnabas, Silas, and many others, who were not apostles, are prominent in this book.

The genre of the book of Acts is Narrative History with several Sermons. Luke, the author of the Gospel of Luke, was a doctor and Gentile. He wrote this book circa 60-62 A.D. It is Luke's sequel to the Gospel of Luke.

☂ BLACK Fact:

The book of Genesis records that Noah has three sons named Shem, Ham, and Japheth. (Gen. 5:32) The name Ham literally means black. Many Bible scholars and some anthropologists consider Ham to be the father of Negroes, Mongoloids, and Indians.

It is titled "Acts" to emphasize that this book records the "Acts of the Apostles through the work of the "Holy Spirit". The key personalities of Acts are Peter, Paul, John, James, Stephen, Barnabas, Timothy, Lydia, Silas, and Apollos.

Luke wrote the book of Acts (Acts of the Apostles) to record how believers were empowered by the Holy Spirit, worked to spread the Gospel of Christ, and is a model for the future church.

The book of Acts is also the history of the birth, the founding, and the spread of the Church from Jerusalem to Rome. It also records the transition of the Church from being almost exclusively a Jewish institution into becoming a Gentile and an international institution. Consequently, it records the transition of Christianity from a Jewish religion into an international faith. The Gospel of salvation is for all because Jesus Christ is Lord of all.

• Chapters 1-6:7, contains the events that surround Jerusalem and the infancy of the church. The contents of these passages surround the early evangelistic work in Jerusalem. It describes the events of Pentecost, and the amazingly bold sermon presented by the Apostle Peter to all the Jews who gathered for the Feast of Weeks. The result of this sermon was 3000 new believers surrendering to Jesus Christ.

- In chapters 6:8-9:31, there is a shift in the focus of evangelism to other areas. Although the ministry continued in Jerusalem, witnessing the Gospel also included those who were not completely Jewish (Samaritans and Proselytes). In 8:5, Philip traveled down to Samaria, "and began proclaiming Christ to them". Stephen is falsely accused and stoned to death while he preaches to the religious leaders. In Bible History, Stephen was a man of "firsts." He was one of the first seven Christian deacons, and he is generally regarded as the first Christian martyr.

The seven deacons were chosen to assist The Twelve in the service of the new church in Jerusalem. The account is found in Acts 6:1-5:

"Now in these days when the disciples were increasing in number, the Hellenists murmured against the

Hebrews because their widows were neglected in the daily distribution. And the twelve summoned the body of the disciples and said, "It is not right that we should give up preaching the word of God to serve tables. Therefore, brethren, pick out from among you seven men of good repute, full of the Spirit and of wisdom, whom we may appoint to this duty. But we will devote ourselves to prayer and to the ministry of the word." And what they said pleased the whole multitude, and they chose Stephen, a man full of faith and of the Holy Spirit, and Philip, and Prochorus, and Nicanor, and Timon, and Parmenas, and Nicolaus, a proselyte of Antioch."

There was no doubt as to Stephen's exceptionally good character, and the miraculous power that he had been given by God. It's interesting to note that although Stephen was "just" a deacon, he certainly had gifts and powers from God that were at least equal to that of the apostles:

"And Stephen, full of grace and power, did great wonders and signs among the people" (Acts 6:8 RSV)

As had happened with Jesus Christ Himself, Stephen soon found himself in difficulty with the local religious authorities, not because he was doing anything wrong, but because he was seen as a serious and growing threat to their misguided control over the people. They just couldn't "compete" with him:

"They could not withstand the wisdom and the Spirit with which he spoke." (Acts 6:10 RSV)

They then resorted to the "low as you can go" approach; they had him falsely accused of blasphemy - and in knowingly doing so, they themselves blasphemed the Holy Spirit, which was actually the source of Stephen's wisdom

"Then they secretly instigated men, who said, "We have heard him speak blasphemous words against Moses and God ... and set up false witnesses who said, "This man never ceases to speak words against this holy place and the law; for we have heard him say that this Jesus of Nazareth [see

Nazarene] will destroy this place, and will change the customs which Moses delivered to us." (Acts 6:11, 13-14 RSV)

Stephen was arrested and brought before the Sanhedrin where more false accusations were made. While the despicable lies were being spewed at him, Stephen remained calm:

"And gazing at him, all who sat in the council saw that his face was like the face of an angel." (Acts 6:15 RSV)

Stephen was then allowed to make his "defense." By then, he probably knew full well that he was not going to get out of there alive, so he held nothing back out of concern to not offend people that he would otherwise have been gently, tactfully and systematically leading to the Truth, point by point, day by day - had time permitted. The result was one of the most direct, nonpolitical, and beautifully logical historical and theological discourses in The Holy Bible. It's found in its entirety in Acts chapter 7. Every word that he spoke was the Truth, which of course only made his accusers, who were self-righteous hypocrites, hate him all the more. His words of Truth turned them from a pack of petty liars into a raving lynch mob (Acts 7:54).

Stephen was dragged out of the city, where they began stoning him. To keep their clothes from becoming splattered with Stephen's blood during the murder, they "laid down their garments at the feet of a young man named Saul" (Acts 7:58 RSV) - to which Saul, later known as Paul the Apostle, confessed, as written in the opening paragraph.

As Stephen was dying, he prayed to Jesus Christ, "Lord Jesus, receive my spirit!" (7:59). Saul spent his early days oppressing Christians and imprisoning them, until he had a life changing experience with Jesus Christ on the road to Damascus in chapter 9:3.

- From chapters 9:32-12:24, evangelism of the gospel among the gentiles begins. Peter received a revelation that the gospel was also to be shared among the Gentiles. Cornelius, a Roman Commander and some of his men become followers of Christ. Saul (the persecutor) has become a passionate follower of Christ and immediately begins preaching the gospel. We also find that the term "Christians" is first used in Antioch.

- In 12:25-16:5 the gospel is shared geographically to the Gentiles in a different region farther outside Jerusalem. Saul changes his Hebrew name to Paul, a Greek name, to reach the Gentiles. Paul and Barnabas begin their first and second missionary journeys to the Gentile world with both success and opposition. In chapter 15, the Jerusalem Council takes place to authorize spreading the gospel message to the Gentile nations.

- From 16:6-19:20, after they are forbidden to enter Asia, Paul receives a vision. He and Silas head farther West to

Macedonia to preach the gospel message in the Gentile European regions. Lydia, a woman who sold purple fabric, became the first convert along with her entire household. Paul preached to the Greek philosophers on Mars Hill and next sets out on his third missionary journey. "The word of the Lord was growing mightily and prevailing," (19:20).

- The final chapters from 19:21-28, describe Paul's travel to Jerusalem where he was arrested, and then his difficult travel to Rome to be put on trial. When he arrives, he is imprisoned in house arrest and the book of Acts abruptly ends without describing the events of his trial before Caesar.

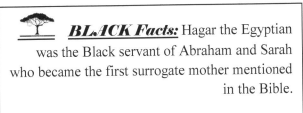

BLACK Facts: Hagar the Egyptian was the Black servant of Abraham and Sarah who became the first surrogate mother mentioned in the Bible.

Let's look deeper by picking up at chapter 3. Chapter 3 opens at the Beautiful Gate of the Temple, where Peter healed a man who had been lame from birth. This miracle attracted the attention of the Jewish leaders and started real opposition to the Christian movement. When a large crowd gathered around the healed man, Peter took advantage of the situation and preached another sermon.

In Chapter 4, we find the first persecution of Christ's followers. Opponents of Jesus had killed Him, thinking that would be the end of the problems He had caused them. To their surprise, their problems were just beginning. So, these religious leaders begin to threaten and suppress Jesus followers. As Peter and John preach to the people at Solomon's porch in Chapter 4, the authorities arrive. Because the Sadducees do not want anyone to preach about the resurrection of Jesus, they have the apostles arrested.

Peter and John's trial is held the next day before Annas the high priest. The members of the Sanhedrin ignore the facts of the resurrection and simply tell Peter and John to cease their preaching (4:5-21). After being released, Peter and John tell their friends what has happened, and they all join in prayer. In their prayer, Peter and John ask God for the grace to speak His word boldly and without fear.

In Chapter 5, we find that Satan is not only at work outside the church in the form of persecution, but inside the church through deception. This fact is illustrated in the story of Ananias and Sapphira, who wanted glory without paying the price. Coveting the plaudits of men was evidence enough that they were operating in the realm of the flesh rather than the Spirit. But that becomes even more obvious to us when we learn that their confidence for the future was in their bank account rather than in the Lord. They could not bear to do what the others were doing—give their substance totally to God and trust solely in His faithfulness to meet their needs. They had to have that money. And these two expressions of fleshliness, their desire for praise, and their confidence in material things, presented them with a difficult dilemma. How could they get the congratulations they craved from the congregation without laying everything on the altar of sacrifice? They finally came up with a solution. Fake it!

"But a certain man named Ananias, with his wife Sapphira, sold a piece of property, and kept back some of the price for himself, with his wife's full knowledge, and bringing a portion of it, he laid it at the apostles' feet" (Acts 5:1, 2). They collaborated on a plan to stash some of the money from the sale of their property in a safety deposit box for themselves and take the rest to the apostles. They would not necessarily say they were giving all of the money they received from the sale; they would just let everyone assume that. And presto, they would have instant acclaim as spiritual, self-sacrificing believers who had surrendered everything to Jesus Christ.

What was so wrong with their plan? They did not really lie to anybody, did they? They just gave the money and said nothing about what percentage of the total sale price it represented. They could not help what other people thought, could they? Evidently they could. Peter, with miraculous divine discernment, attributed their scheme to Satan and called it lying to the Holy Spirit (Acts 5:3). He explained that they were under no obligation to sell their property. And even after they sold it, they were under no obligation to give all the money to the church. But they *were* obligated to be honest (Acts 5:4).

The major sin of Ananias and Sapphira was dishonesty, deceit, hypocrisy, pretense, presenting a false image of themselves, implying a greater spirituality than they actually possessed, letting people think more highly of them than what they knew was warranted. They were more interested in *appearances* than in *reality*. Peter said, "You have not lied to men, but to God" (Acts 5:4).

The church has had hypocrites from the very beginning. They are Satan's way of attacking the church from the inside. The problem of discrimination arises in Chapter 6. We find Satan busy trying to break the fellowship of the church. How do the apostles work out a solution to this potential problem? According to Acts 6:3; "Brothers, choose from among you seven men who are respected and who are full of the Holy Spirit and wisdom. We will have them take care of this work." (NLV) This then stops the inherent complications of confusion that the enemy so happily uses as a weapon.

Books of the Old Testament

32 Authors
3600 Years of Man's History
1500 Years in Writing

Law
5

- Genesis
- Exodus
- Leviticus
- Numbers
- Deuteronomy

History
12

- Joshua
- Judges
- Ruth
- I Samuel
- II Samuel
- I Kings
- II Kings
- I Chronicles
- II Chronicles
- Ezra
- Nehemiah
- Esther

Poetry
5

- Job
- Psalms
- Proverbs
- Ecclesiastes
- The Song of Solomon

Prophecy
17

- Isaiah
- Jeremiah
- Lamentations
- Ezekiel
- Daniel
- Hosea
- Joel
- Amos
- Obadiah
- Jonah
- Micah
- Nahum
- Habakkuk
- Zephaniah
- Haggai
- Zechariah
- Malachi

"For the prophecy came not in old time by the will of man: but holy men of God spake as they were moved by the Holy Ghost" 2 Peter 1:21

The Time Periods

Innocence   Conscience   Patriarchs   Law

Why was Saul going to Damascus? (9:2)

_____

What did he see near Damascus? (9:3)

_____

When the disciples in Jerusalem were afraid to accept Paul, who spoke up in his defense? (9:27)

_____

_____

Who saw a vision in which an angel spoke to him? (10:1-4)

_____

Answer the following questions from chapter 13-28:

Where did Paul's first missionary journey start?

_____

Who were his companions? (12:25)

_____

Who was Paul's companion on the second journey? (15:40)

_____

What happened to Barnabas? (15:36-39)

_____

Who joined the journey? (16:1)

_____

What happened at Philippi: (16:12-15)

_____

What happened in Athens? (17:22-31)

_____

Where did Paul go on his third journey? (18:23)

_____

Paul says his last farewell to his friends at Ephesus and then sails to Jerusalem for the last time.

What is he accused of: (21:27-28)

_____

Who is Felix? (24:10-21)

_____

At his trial, Paul appeals to Caesar and chapter 26 records Pau's defense before King Agrippa after which Paul is taken as a prisoner to Rome to made his appeal to Caesar.

What kind of trip did he have? (27:1-28:15)

_____

Paul is put under house arrest in Rome for two more years, during which he writes *Philemon, Colossians, Ephesians, Philippians, and II Timothy.* Tradition says that Paul is later condemned and beheaded.

The Book of Acts ends abruptly, but the church goes on. The heroes that lost their lives in this book each contributed to the spreading of the Gospel. We are not writing the 29th chapter of Acts. WHAT WILL WE DO?

Cheat Sheet
General Review of the Period

Clement was the leading elder in Rome in 150 who in order to restore harmony to the church demanded obedience to the Deacons and Elders. The oldest sermon after the Apostles was the 2nd Book of Clement. Ignatius, the Bishop from Antioch was the first to promulgate the Power of Bishops.

The apologists were the defenders against the attack on Christianity between 140 and 200. Justin Martyr spent his life to prove Christianity was around long before other histories. Christianity was defended against atheism, cannibalism, immorality and antisocial action.

Tertullian is credited with writing the Vulgate which became the basis for Roman Catholic Theology.

The Polemicists were the defenders of Christianity against heresy. The only source for true doctrine was the New Testament. People who fell out during persecution could not be forgiven by the Church only by God.

Identify Gnostics – Mystical, religions & philosophical doctrine combining Christianity Greek and Oriental Philosophy.

Their one impact on the church was rise of Bishops as defenders of the Faith.

In 262, the Montanist Error taught the following things that were to tear the church asunder:

1. End of world at hand – coming to end.
2. Age of Holy Spirit – fasting, celibacy, strict moral discipline.

In extremes caused the church to condemn them and declare Biblical revelation had come to an end. Spiritual gifts were no longer in operation.

Novation, in 252 caused the following to happen what was to split the church for 3 centuries.

1. Defender of Doctrine of Trinity
2. Church could not restore anyone
3. Purist concept of Church membership

Manicheism was:

> Ancient dualist belief system; a religious doctrine based on the separation of matter and spirit and of good and evil that originated in 3rd century Persia and combined elements of Zoroastrianism, Buddhism, Christianity, and Gnosticism

The following heresies crept into the church:

1. Greatest enemy – Internal fighting

2. Ebionism – Continued Jewish opposition to Paul

3. Galatians – Rebuked salvation through law keeping; men saved by good works

4. Lawkeepers – Circumcision and Sabbath keeping

5. Gnosticism – ordinary man could get salvation by faith and good works only elite had chance at spiritual salvation

Medieval Papacy

In its beginning (I Timothy 3:1; Acts 20:38) – Bishop, elder, deacon were the same

Define Bishop – overseer or pastor of a single congregation

Iraneus taught that the church at Rome was established by Peter and Paul and they were successors.

In the 3rd Century, Cyprian the Bishop at Carthage taught universal church outside of which there is no salvation, ruled by bishops who were successors to the apostles. It became the law.

TIMELINE OF THE ANCIENT CHURCH

The Apostles	The Apostolic Fathers	The Apologists	The Thoelogians
•A.D. 100	•A.D. 150	•A.D. 300	•A.D. 600

𝔅lacks in the 𝔅ook of 𝔄cts

- *Acts 2:9-10 The Jewish pilgrims gathered at Pentecost included persons of African descent, notably the Elamites of Mesopotamia and those from Egypt, Libya, and Cyrene.*

- *Acts 8:26-40 The Ethiopian Finance Minister on a mission for the Queen of the Ethiopians, the Kandake or Candace; he is baptized as perhaps the first non-Jew (an early tradition that rivals the baptism of Cornelius).*

- *Acts 13:1 Two of the four prophets and teachers at Antioch (where persons of the Way were first called Christians-- 11:26) were Africans, namely Lucius of Cyrene and Simeon who was called Niger, a Latinism for "the Black Man."*

- *Acts 18:24,25 Apollos, the Jew of Alexandria in North Africa, becomes converted (1 Corinthians 3).*

Part 2

Our Church in History

1. **Waldo or Valdez and the Waldenses (1176 AD).**
   The "Best Way To God".
   Aim: To seek to understand certain trends in the belief and practices of the Waldenses and their possible relation to later Pentecostal beliefs and practices.

2. **The Huguenots and the Wars of Religion (1562 to 1594 AD).** In the convents of Southern France.
   Aim: To seek to understand the relation, if one exists, between the persecution of the Huguenots and reassertion of the charismatic dynamic among them.

3. **George Fox (1642 – 1645 AD).** In search of Spiritual Reality.
   Aim: To seek to understand the perils of religious formalism and its inability to bind the seeking, longing spirit for wholeness.

4. **Mother Ann Lee.** An instance of Spirit and Establishmentarian conflict.

Aim: To see and understand a case of glossolalia in terms of the freedom of the spirit and the laws of the establishment.

5. **John Wesley.** The case of the absence of charismatic activity.

   Aim: To appreciate Wesley's insight concerning the reasons for the absence of spiritual gifts in the churches.

6. **The Holiness Movement:** Parent of the Pentecostal Movement.

   Aim: To seek to understand the rise of the Holiness Movement and how it created the climate out of which Pentecostalism of the 20th Century was born.

7. **Charles Fox Parham.** Bethel Bible College, Topeka, Kansas. The beginning of the Pentecostal Movement in the 20th Century.

   Aim: To understand the ministry of Charles Fox Parham, Particularly as it relates to the outpouring of the Spirit and the subsequent involvement of William J. Seymour.

8. **Williams J. Seymour.** The man behind the Movement.

   Aim: To understand how Azusa Street set the foundation of where we are in the church world today.

The Medieval Period extended from the late 400s to the late 1300s CE (around 900 years). Medieval civilization was created by a combining of three primary elements: Judeo- Christian religion and values, Classical (Greco-Roman) civilization and barbarian culture. To a lesser extent, the neighboring cultures of the Byzantine east and Muslim Spain also made contributions to Medieval Civilization.

The Fall of Rome. Roman Civilization began to deteriorate from about 200 CE onward, though in the Fourth Century (300s) there were several successful turnarounds of this trend. In the late 400s the weakness of the Empire, caused by corruption and various other stresses, combined with barbarian pressure from the northeast, causing a catastrophic collapse of the Roman government. The eastern portion

> **BLACK Facts:**
>
> Phinehas, the grandson of Aaron and a high priest (Exodus 6:25). The name, Phinehas, is Egyptian and means literally, "The Nubian," or "The Dark-skinned One."

of the Empire continued until the 1450s as the Byzantine Empire with its own Greek-based civilization.

The Dark Age. The collapse of Roman civilization in western Europe was followed by a Dark Age of barbarian invasion, settlement and supremacy, lasting around 300 years. The new barbarian kingdoms included Visigoths (Spain), Ostrogoths (Italy), Lombards (Italy), Franks (France) and the Anglo-Saxon kingdoms in Britain. These Germanic kingdoms all eventually converted to Catholic Christianity and formed an alliance with the Church. The main civilizing factors during this dark period were the Christian Church and the manorial system.

- The Church preserved learning and the arts, mainly in the cathedral cities and in monastic houses, which began to form after the year 500. It also supplied strong leadership and organization during the dark years of chaos and deterioration.

- Manorialism was built around the nucleus of wealthy and powerful estates, called manors, which usually contained a fortified villa and surrounding lands with the associated industries. Together, these elements formed a unit which was virtually self-contained.

The Holy Roman Empire. The Frankish kingdom which replaced much of the former Roman province of Gaul, was at first ruled by a line of kings founded by the warlord Clovis and known as the Merovingian Dynasty.

Several centuries later, the Frankish kingdom became the model for the formation of medieval Europe through the leadership of Charles the Great. Charles conquered the nearby lands of the Lombards and Saxons as well as aiding the Christian rulers of northern Spain in pushing the Muslims further south. He was an able administrator and kept his diverse kingdom together through tight organization and supervision. Charles fostered a renewal of the arts and learning, known as the Carolingian Renaissance. For his successes and service to the Church, Charles was crowned Holy Roman Emperor in the year 800.

Charles' success in reuniting a considerable portion of Rome's former territory caused some people to hope that Rome could be revived permanently. Charles' Holy Roman Empire began to weaken, however, during the final years of his reign and, in the time of his grandsons, was divided into three portions. In the late 800s the Carolingian attempt at reviving Rome's empire was much reduced and fragmented, so that by the Tenth Century, Europe was again in survival mode as Magyars, Turks and Vikings raided, settled and spread havoc.

> ### *Black Facts:*
> The Queen of Sheba ruled a kingdom that included territory in both Arabia and Africa. When she visited Solomon, she was accorded the dignity and status of a head of state (1 Kings 10:1-13).

In this new situation, leadership was not provided by kings, but by local nobles who ruled their domains semi-independently. The exception to this rule was Tenth Century Germany, where Otto I dominated his nobles and recreated a version of the Holy Roman Empire for a time, until the nobility was able to re-assert control over their own domains.

The system under which order was established and maintained is known as feudalism. Lords awarded portions of land, called fiefs, to noblemen in exchange for oaths of loyalty and service. These men were called vassals and ruled their fiefs and the serfs (peasants and common people) living on them. Noblemen often served as heavy cavalry, or knights, in the service of a lord or vassal. In time, knights developed a code of warfare and behavior, called chivalry (the code of the horseman), in which the ideal Christian gentleman lived in courtesy, honor and religious devotion.

The High Middle Ages. By the Eleventh Century, strong leadership and stability began to re-emerge in several places, notably France and England. For example, in 1066 Duke William of Normandy invaded Britain and conquered the Anglo-Saxon Kingdom, making himself king. He awarded fiefs to his Norman and French knights, largely replacing the Anglo-Saxon nobility. His strong central government made Norman England the most stable kingdom in Europe.

The time between 1000 and 1300 are often thought of as the High Middle Ages. During these years, kings and nobles provided enough stability so that people could think beyond simple survival. New land was reclaimed from swamps, forests (and in Holland, even from the sea). Agricultural production increased. Trade flourished. Trade guilds were formed to regulate commerce and ensure the rights of merchants and tradesmen. New products were introduced from the Middle East and beyond. Large annual trade fairs were established throughout Europe. Coinage began to replace barter as the means of exchange. Castle building made attacks on neighboring lands difficult and costly. Technology advanced, along with basic civic planning.

During this time, the Papacy and the Catholic Church rose to a height of power and prestige. Popes and clergy could enforce their will upon nobles through the threat of excommunication. From Rome, the Vatican administered a vast empire including most of Western Europe. Gothic architecture expressed worship through ambitious new designs and building techniques. Catholics from across Europe were able to unite around the common venture of the Crusades (1099 – 1297).

Scholasticism. Re-contact with the Byzantine East and the Muslim world during the Crusades, the writings of the ancient Greeks, especially Aristotle, were re-discovered, studied and debated. Scholars were attracted to the life of learning, centered around major cathedrals. This advance in scholarship developed into scholasticism, which attempted to understand and explore all subject areas under the guidance of theology. Jewish scholasticism (Maimonides) and Muslim scholasticism (Averroes) interacted and argued with Catholic scholastics, like Thomas Aquinas, over the meaning and application of Aristotelian thought to contemporary issues.

Christian scholastics debated whether Aristotle and other Greek thinkers could be helpful (or even compatible) with Christian thought and teachings. Major universities, such as Oxford, Cambridge and Paris were founded through the work of the scholastics.

BLACK Facts: In the Gospel of Matthew, we find the quotation from Hosea 11:1 which reads, "out of Egypt I called my son." The passage is part of the notorious "Flight into Egypt" that describes the way in which Mary and Joseph fled to Egypt to hide the one that King Herod feared would displace him. Assuming that we can lend some historical credence to this report, it is difficult imagining, if the holy family were indeed persons who looked like typical "Europeans," that they could effectively "hide" in Africa. One must remember and take most seriously the fact that Egypt has always been and remains part of Africa. Her indigenous people are noticeably different from the European types, notwithstanding the Hellenistic cultural incursions, beginning in earnest just over 300 B.C. In fact, it has only been in recent centuries that the Egyptians and other North Americans have been officially racially classified as "Caucasian." Nevertheless, for thousands of years, Africans have migrated out of biblical Ethiopia and Egypt and have passed through Palestine en route to the Fertile Crescent or Mesopotamia. Thus, the term Afro-Asiatic emerged, and it is a fitting description of persons from Abraham to Jesus and his disciples.

During the High Middle Ages, feudalism began to lose its important function as the basis for society. Cities were re-invigorated and began to expand. Peasants began to leave the land, moving to cities to find a new life. Strong kings and nobles could afford to raise standing armies through tax revenues. This allowed kings to be less dependent upon vassals for military support, enabling them to gain greater control over their domains.

The Late Middle Ages. The Fourteenth Century saw several setbacks to the progress of the High Middle Ages. The Hundred Years' War between England and France (1337-1453) drained both countries of resources. The ravages of the Bubonic Plague (1347 – 1350) killed between a quarter and a third of Europe's population. These things, along with series of serious natural disasters, caused the population of Europe to decrease and social progress to slow down drastically.

In this period, the power of the nobility was reduced as kings imposed their will and made alliances with the merchants of the growing middle class. These strong central governments gave rise to the nations of modern Europe. At the same time, the power and prestige of the Papacy was damaged by popular reaction to the set-backs of the later crusades and by the refusal of kings to be intimidated by Vatican threats of excommunication. Movements like the one led by Francis of Assisi to criticize the wealth of the Catholic Church, began a rethinking of Christian practice and church allegiance. The revival of the classical viewpoint known as humanism began to take hold in the universities and other places as theological views were questioned and debated. This would give rise to the humanistic Renaissance beginning around 1400 in Italy.

The Middle Ages came to a close through the innovations of Renaissance, the discovery and exploration of the Americas and the drastic rethinking of Christianity in the Protestant Reformation. By the mid 1400s, with the Renaissance in full bloom, the Middle Ages would effectively come to an end.

> *BLACK Facts:* Ebed-melech ("Royal Servant"), the Ethiopian. He was an officer of King Zedekiah who, at great risk to himself, saved Jeremiah's life (Jeremiah 38:7-13)., and was blessed by Jeremiah (Jeremiah 39:15-18).

Africa during the Middle Ages

Medieval Europe was familiar with Egypt and northern African countries, but the majority of this continent remained a mystery to Middle Age society. South of the Sahara, only limited penetration by Arabs brought back stories of these exotic lands. But civilizations flourished during these centuries, especially in Ghana and along Africa's East Coast.

Traders, merchants and adventurers traditionally used routes established by the Chinese and Arabs based around well-known northern African ports. Some took their wares as far south as the trade winds would allow. The port at Mogadishu became the most important Muslim city on the East Coast. But despite its proximity to Kenya and Tanzania, few attempts were made to bring this thriving culture inland.

Medieval Europe's nearly unquenchable thirst for gold led to some expeditions deeper into Africa. One medieval African trade route took travelers through the city of Timbuktu, on their way to the Ivory Coast.

Medieval architecture in Africa was heavily influenced by Islamic styles, and mosques were built at Kilwa and Mogadishu, but early Christianity also had a presence on the continent, most notably in Ethiopia. The Church of St. George at Lalibela is cut directly from a rock wall. Explorations made during the Renaissance would probe deeper into the continent as European countries began to colonize Africa.

1. The great outstanding fact in the ten centuries of the Middle Ages was The development of papa; power

2. Gregory I introduced the Doctrines of adoration of images, purgatory, and transubstantiation. He was a strong advocate of the monastic life.

3. The one steady institution in the upheaval of the empire was the church.

4. Pious Frauds" were the things put forth to support the authority of Rome.

5. The Donation of Constantine was Supreme authority over all European Provinces.

6. The false Decretals of Isidore was the absolute supremacy of the pope of Rome over the universal church – independence of church from state.

7. The main evidences of forgery were from the Latin Vulgate.

8. Hildebrand really ruled the church as the power behind the throne for more than 20 years.

9. The things that Hildebrand did were <u>reformed clergy, lifted standard of morals, compelled the celibacy</u> and freed the church from the <u>domination of the state</u>, and made the <u>church supreme</u>.

10. Pope Innocent III presented that the pope ruled the <u>whole church</u> and the <u>whole world</u>.

1. Describe the Council of Constance: <u>1414 was held to decide between the claims of 4 popes…all were deposed.</u>

2. Islam means <u>"submission"</u> and obedience to <u>will of God</u>.

3. The Mohammedan faith encompasses about <u>600,000,000</u> people.

4. Identify Mohammed: <u>Prophet born in Mecca in 570 A.D. Brought religion and authority of scattered Arabian tribes under authority</u>

5. The doctrines of Mohammed are :

    a. Unity of God – One God

    b. All events, whether good or evil have been foreordained by God

    c. Multitudes of angels dealing with men

    d. God has given revelation in the Koran

e. God sent great prophets – Adam, Moses, Jesus and Mohammed.

f. In hereafter, a final resurrection, judgment and heaven or hell for every man.

16. At first Mohammed relied on <u>moral influences</u>, but soon changed his methods and became a <u>warrior</u>. The alternatives were to accept <u>Islam</u> or <u>death to resistors</u>.

17. All Europe would have been Mohammedan except for the battle of <u>Tours</u>.

18. Islam's' power was so strong because they believed that they were <u>accomplishing the will of God and destined to succeed</u>. Anyone who died with unbelievers entered an immediate heaven of <u>sensual delight</u>. The populations of the Greek Empire were made up of <u>churchmen</u> and <u>monks</u> who were ready to <u>pray</u> but not to <u>fight</u>.

19. The favorable aspects in the religion of Mohammed were:

a. Simplicity of doctrine.

b. Opposition to image worship.

c. Swept away priestly rites – brought every soul face to face with God

d. Abstinence from strong drink.

e. Literature & science promoted.

20. On the other side of the coin, Mohammedianism errors and evils are:

a. Conversion by conquest – promoting hate instead of love.

b. State & church absolutely one/translation of Koran into vernacular.

c. Mohammed conception of God based on Old rather than New Testament.

d. Leaves Christ out of the doctrinal scheme and made him inferior to Mohammed.

e. Conception of heaven totally sensual.

f. Degradation of womanhood (slaves/play things of men).

g. Worst governed lands on earth.

21. The separation of the Latin and Greek churches was formally made in the 11th Century

Latin

Greek

From the father & the Son **The Holy Ghost**

From Father alone

Forbidden/Abstained **Marriage**

Must even for Village priests

Adoration practiced **Images**

Only pictures – no adoration

Used water **Communion**

Common bread

Wanted to dominate **Politics**

Church and state separate

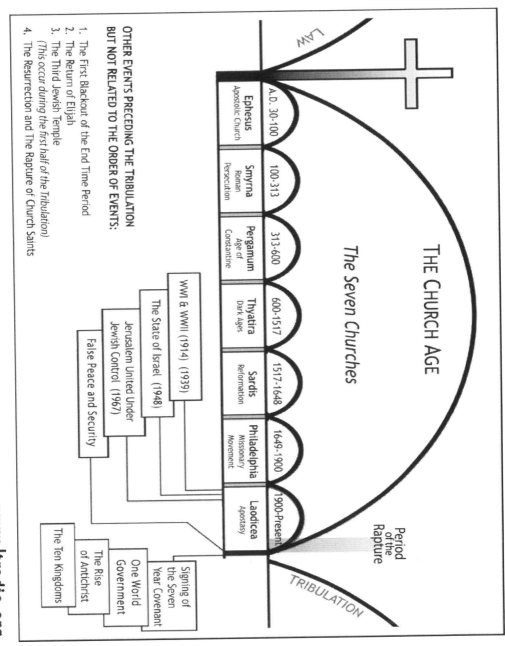

THE CHURCH AGE

The Seven Churches

LAW

Ephesus Apostolic Church	A.D. 30-100
Smyrna Roman Persecution	100-313
Pergamum Age of Constantine	313-600
Thyatira Dark Ages	600-1517
Sardis Reformation	1517-1648
Philadelphia Missionary Movement	1649-1900
Laodicea Apostasy	1900-Present

Period of the Rapture

TRIBULATION

WWI & WWII (1914) (1939)

The State of Israel (1948)

Jerusalem United Under Jewish Control (1967)

False Peace and Security

Signing of the Seven Year Covenant

The Rise of Antichrist

One World Government

The Ten Kingdoms

OTHER EVENTS PRECEDING THE TRIBULATION BUT NOT RELATED TO THE ORDER OF EVENTS:

1. The First Blackout of the End Time Period
2. The Return of Elijah
3. The Third Jewish Temple
   (This occur during the first half of the Tribulation)
4. The Resurrection and The Rapture of Church Saints

www.ltradio.org

61 | P a g e

2. Analyze each crusade in one statement.

First one – Two parts – Peter Hermit went on faith – wiped out / Godfrey took city of Jerusalem in 1099 – Feudal kingdom

Second one – Bernard – many defeats – held off fall of kingdom

Third one – Richard "lionhearted" – pilgrims gained right to visit the Holy Sepulchre unmolested

Fourth one – Worse than a failure – really hurt church

Fifth one – Jerusalem Bethlehem, Nazareth – ceded to Christianity

Sixth one – Luis IX – Defeated by Mohammedans

Seventh one – Failure

3. Name the three causes of failure of the crusades.
   1. Constant quarrelling among the leaders
   2. No vision of how to really run a kingdom
   3. Conquest was an intrusion, not a liberation

4. List the 5 good causes of the Crusades
   1. Pilgrims were protected and land prospered
   2. Moslem progression checked
   3. Nations became better acquainted with each other

4. Crusades furnished a great impulse to trade

5. Ecclesiastical power greatly increased

5. In the long run, what was the final result?

The vast wealth, overwhelming ambition, unscrupulous use of power by churchmen aroused discontent and paved way for revolt against Catholic Church

6. Identify Monasticism and the three mail rules.

The concept of living apart from the world.

   a.   Obedience to head of mastery

   b.   Poverty or possession of no property

   c.   Personal chastity

7. List the seven benefits of monasticism and the 4 evils.

Seven benefits:

   i. Center for peace and quiet

   ii. Hospitality to sick and poor

   iii. Refuge to helpless

   iv. Promoted agriculture

   v. Preserved literature

   vi. Were educators

   vii. Early missionaries

Four evils:

i. Promulgated celibate life as highest form: unnatural and unscriptural

ii. Secluded multitudes from family, social, civic and national life

iii. Luxury – led to lax discipline, idleness, open immorality

iv. Contributions extorted from rich families

8. Why was this period called the Dark Ages?

Monasteries at lowest esteem of people – great minds were locked up in the church.

9. Give one statement about each of the following:

Albigenes – Puritans-Pure New Testamentalist – Opposed Catholic Church

Waldensians – Preached scriptures again

Roman Catholics – Established order of Evangelists

John Wycliff – Movement in England for Reformation. Translated the Bible into English.

John Huss – Proclaimed freedom from Papal authority – burned at stake

Jerome Savonarola – Preached Reformation – Hanged and burned by Pope

Peter Abelard – Boldest thinker of Middle Ages – married – forced to separate.

Bernard of Clairvaux – promoted second crusade – wrote songs – "Jesus Very Thought of Thee".

Thomas Aquinas – Most celebrated and highest authority of all medieval period in philosophy and theology.

10. Why was the fall of Constantinople so important?

1453 – Dividing point between Medieval and Modern times.

BLACK

Facts: The Ethiopian, Taharqa, spelled Tirhakah in the Bible. When Hezekiah revolted against Assyria in 705 B.C., he did so with the support of Shaboka and Shebitku (702-690), rulers of the Twenty-fifth Dynasty of Egypt. Tirhakah led an army in support of Judah during Hezekiah's revolt against Assyria (2 Kings 19:9; Isaiah 37:9). Tirhakah later ruled Egypt from 690-664

The following is taken from the Christian Reformed Church In North America website (www.crcna.org)

What sets the Christian Reformed Church off from many other denominations is its embrace of key teachings of John Calvin. In a nutshell, these all center on the sovereignty of God. The biblical teachings of predestination and election give us comfort because they assure us that no one and nothing, not even our own bad choices, can snatch us out of God's hand. And the realization that God owns all of creation and continues to assert his rule over it gives us a sure hope for the future.

John Calvin's teachings blossomed in many countries, including the Netherlands. While much of the Netherlands remained Roman Catholic, the Reformed faith established itself as the state church. As is often the case, politics and church make a bad mix. The Reformed Church in the Netherlands began to show its share of moral decay and of theological liberalism - the latter largely spurred on by the Enlightenment, an intellectual movement that idolized human reason at the expense of Bible-based faith.

In response to this trend, a grassroots movement developed among the less-educated lower-income folk, who clung to a simple, practical faith based on traditional Calvinist doctrines. Because the churches did not nurture such faith, those who joined this movement worshiped in small groups called "conventicles."

When the Reformed Church began to actively persecute the leaders of this movement, a number of groups, under the leadership of Rev. Hendrik de Cock and others, seceded from the church. This branch of Dutch Calvinism ultimately gave rise to the Christian Reformed Church.

Coming to North America

The next key event that led to the formation of the CRC was the decision of secessionist pastor Albertus Van

Raalte to flee from the specter of religious persecution and famine in the Netherlands. Together with his wife, his family, and some forty others, Van Raalte immigrated to the United States. In 1848, they settled in and around what is now Holland, Michigan, establishing a "colony" on American soil that fervently held onto Calvinist doctrine, practical piety, and a strong commitment to living all of life to the glory of God.

It wasn't easy. Inexperienced and crippled by disease, the settlers faltered under the grueling task of extracting a living from the untamed ground. Only the steady trickle of new immigrants kept their ranks replenished and even allowed for some modest growth in their numbers. Through these first terribly difficult and painful years, the settlers tenaciously clung to their most prized possessions: their faith and the freedom to live out that faith in their daily life.

Separation from the Dutch Reformed Church

The harsh conditions in the fledgling "colony" convinced Van Raalte to seek help from the Dutch Reformed Church. That church had been introduced to American soil over a century before, when Dutch Reformed merchants accompanying Peter Stuyvesant settled in New York, then called New Amsterdam. That line of communication between Van Raalte's Michigan churches and the Dutch Reformed congregations of New Jersey soon blossomed into a full-fledged merger.

In 1857 a small fragment of four churches, about 130 families, seceded from the new union. Among the reasons they cited were:

- a perceived lack of sound doctrinal preaching by American pastors;
- a perceived lack of piety and too much accommodation to American culture by these same pastors;

- the use of hymns in worship by the Americans - the seceders insisted on psalm-singing only;

- the practice by the American churches of "open communion," extending an open invitation to all believers to participate in the Lord's Supper;

- the perceived lack of solidarity on the part of the Americans with the secessionist cause in the Netherlands.

In 1857, the Christian Reformed Church was born.

Abraham Kuyper

The stream of Dutch immigrants into the CRC increased dramatically in the latter part of the nineteenth century. These new arrivals shared a commitment to the Reformed creeds and confessions, but they introduced a very different vision. Their views were shaped largely by the great Dutch theologian and statesman, Dr. Abraham Kuyper.

Won over to the simple, biblically based faith of those who had seceded from the Reformed Church of the Netherlands some fifty years earlier, Kuyper led a movement out of the Reformed Church that joined the seceders. Kuyper's great contribution to the seceder movement, and, through the immigrants, to the Christian Reformed Church, was a more outward-looking faith.

While still solidly grounded in Scripture and the confessions, Kuyper's vision was to claim Christ's lordship over all of life. Believers were not only called to maintain holy lives in relation to God and each other, they were also called to extend God's kingdom into the society in which they lived. Believers were to look beyond the hard, wooden pews and their family altars to take on the world for Christ - using Christian schools, institutions, and organizations to make God's redemptive and recreating work a reality in the marketplace, city hall, and factory.

The new vision that began to live among CRC members did not displace the down-home piety, but it did spur the infant CRC to peer over the walls of its cradle to begin to engage a wider world.

Becoming North American

At the turn of the century the CRC began to make the difficult transition of moving from the Dutch language to English. That did not happen overnight. On the positive side, it meant the CRC could emerge from its isolation, engaging culture and society and forging relationships with other Christians. On the negative side, a major element of the CRC's cohesion began to dissolve. And CRC members, especially the youth, became increasingly vulnerable to the dangers and pitfalls of Americanism.

The First World War accelerated that process. Young CRC soldiers fought for the United States and came back more determined than ever to be Americans. The CRC as a whole supported the war effort, and its members became increasingly loyal to what they began to see as their land.

After the war the CRC had a difficult time defining itself. It wanted to become American but it also wanted to cling tenaciously to its Reformed beliefs and practices, which many felt could only find full expression in Dutch. This led to disagreements, and, in typical Reformed style, to secession. Calvin Seminary Professor Ralph Janssen left the CRC because of sustained investigations into his views on science as a legitimate source of knowledge that could contribute positively to Christians' understanding of the world. Herman Hoeksema's rejection of "common grace" sparked the secession of the Protestant Reformed Church from the CRC.

The Depression years were difficult for CRC members. The church had spread in pockets throughout the United States. The rigors of survival caused them to look more inward than outward. As a result they were losing touch with each other and with their roots. Banner editor H.J.

Kuiper sounded the alarm, encouraging members to dedicate themselves afresh to the Reformed faith. Kuiper identified three factions in the CRC that we can still identify to some extent today: those who cling tenaciously to historical Calvinism, those who espouse a sort of fundamental evangelicalism, and those who follow behind the liberal, socializing, modernistic churches of North America.

The Canadians

The Second World War served to Americanize the CRC even further. But it also had the effect of spurring a new immigration of Dutch Calvinists - this time mostly to Canada. While CRC churches had been planted decades earlier in places like Nobleford and Edmonton, Alberta, new churches sprang up overnight in Alberta, Ontario, Manitoba, and British Columbia.

The large immigration of Dutch Calvinists to Canada in the early 1950s brought some significant culture clash into the CRC. While the Dutch Canadians shared a commitment to the Reformed confessions, they differed from their American cousins in life experience, mindset, and moral and religious values. Dutch Canadians tended to focus their spiritual energies on working out the social ramifications of the gospel, not on personal piety. Yet both groups shared a genuine desire and commitment to remain obedient to God's Word - a solid foundation on which to build a bi-national church.

The Sixties

The flood of changes in values, lifestyles, and social interactions precipitated in the 1960s profoundly affected the CRC. Tidier patterns of church life gave way to a rising disenchantment and disagreement over how believers should respond to the social chaos around them. While the CRC never overtly held racist teachings, members debated long and hard over the ways the church should combat racism - if at all. Even among Kuyperians there was strong disagreement over the extent to which the institutional church should become involved in significant social issues.

The role of women in church leadership also became a hotly contested conflict during the sixties. Changing roles for women in the larger society forced the CRC to ask whether women should be allowed to serve in ecclesiastical office. While both sides in this struggle sincerely sought to be biblically obedient and Reformed in their interpretation of the Scriptures, neither side was able to convince the other. The impasse has led to a compromise decision that allows individual churches to ordain women as elders and classes (if they so choose) to allow their constituent congregations to ordain women as ministers of the Word as well. That decision spurred the departure of more than forty thousand members from the CRC.

Called to Serve

Despite the deeply divisive spirit that has caused such pain in the CRC, there have been many evidences of God's grace as well. People on both sides have reached out in forgiveness and love. While some have left the CRC over their disagreements, many others have stayed. And they continue to be committed to living together and working together in this part of the Body of Christ. Despite the variety of different positions and viewpoints held by members of the CRC, the denomination is still bound together by a deep commitment to respond to the good news that our world belongs to - and is being redeemed by - our faithful God. In the unity and

BLACK Facts: Acts 13:1 Two of the four prophets and teachers at Antioch (where persons of the Way were first called Christians--11:26) were Africans, namely Lucius of Cyrene and Simeon who was called Niger, a Latinism for "the Black Man."

empowerment of that conviction, CRC members join together in an amazing variety and scope of ministries

	Calvinism Tulip	Arminian Response	PCE
T	Total Depravity, no free will, faith to regeneraton is a gift	free will to choose good over evil, may accept or reject regeneraton, Faith is the sinner's gift to God	Total depravity ie unable to save ourselves, faith is a gift, no free will on earth
U	Unconditional election: before the creation of the spirits, for no revealed reason,	Universal Redemption or General Atonement: Christ died for all men. Until the sinner responds, the Spirit cannot give life.	Election was promised before our true free will choices to those who accepted HIS will, and fulfilled after their true free will choice. The gospel was promised before the choice to any elect who fell into sin.
L	Limited atonement, Christ died for elect only	Unlimited atonement: Christ died for the world.	Christ died for the sinful elect only.
I	Irresistible grace. When God has chosen to save someone, He will.	Prevenient grace: must be accepted by free will.	Irresistible grace. God's salvation of the fallen elect is based upon HIS promise before our true free will choice.
P	Perseverence of the saints: Once Saved, Always Saved or OSAS.	Conditional Perseverance believes that salvation is dependent upon faith.	Perseverence of the saints or Once Elect, Always Saved, OEAS

forum link: [IMG]http://i45.tinypic.com/20h0tjs.jpg[/IMG]

5 Factors in the Current Rise of Reformed Theology Among African Americans

Reformed theology is nothing new. So why do more African Americans seem to be adopting it now?

We see evidence of Reformed teaching gaining traction in the African American community through organizations like the Reformed African American Network (RAAN), authors like Anthony Carter and Trillia Newbell, and urban conferences such as Legacy. But Reformed theology has been part of the Black church tradition since the days of slavery. However, as Thabiti Anyabwile observes in his book *The Decline of African American Theology*, African Americans were often prevented from acquiring formal education, so they haven't always used academic and theological categories to express their religious beliefs. Nevertheless, ideas emphasized in Reformed theology — God's sovereignty, the authority of the Bible, and God's faithfulness — have long been hallmarks of the historic Black church. Even where theological jargon was absent, these ideas have been captured in the sermons of Black preachers, sung in Negro spirituals, and visible in the traditions of the African American church.

So why, then, have the formal categories of Reformed theology become more commonly circulated among African Americans in recent years? Here are five attempts to answer that question.

1.) Christian Hip-Hop

The musical genre of hip-hop has long connected with an African American, urban, and youthful crowd. Christian hip-hop (CHH) artists, many of whom have Reformed leanings, have successfully paired infectious beats with transformational truths of the gospel and reached new segments of the population. At the vanguard of CHH is Lecrae, who has achieved cross-over success with two Grammy nominations, a #1 album on iTunes, and a free mixtape with more than 280,000 downloads.

2.) The Digital Age

With the stroke of a key, the click of a button, or the tap of a screen, anyone can access a host of content from many of the most gifted preachers and teachers. African Americans have learned Reformed theology through radio ministries, sermon podcasts, or seminary courses. Never has it been easier for anyone, at any time, and in any place to hear the best of Reformed theology.

3.) Greater Access to Reformed Education

No longer are African Americans forbidden by legal or social barriers to attend schools that teach Reformed theology. This is not to say that all obstacles have disappeared. The United States has not "arrived" in terms of racial and ethnic equality. However, there has been progress. Daniel Aleshire, president

of the Association of Theological Schools, indicates that
African Americans are represented in seminary in proportions
close to the U.S. population. Some Reformed schools even
have specific programs to engage ethnic minorities.

4.) Hunger for Biblical Teaching

All Christians who "taste and see that the Lord is good"
develop a hunger for solid spiritual food. Many African
Americans looking for rich, biblical teaching have found a
home in Reformed theology.

By highlighting historic creeds, influential theologians,
majestic hymns, exegetical preaching, and carefully crafted
systems of thought, Reformed theology has conveyed the
splendor of God to countless Christians for centuries. African
Americans are no exception. As one person commented on
RAAN, "Once I was exposed to the doctrines of grace, I
realized the depth of the true gospel and my need for a deeper
relationship with Christ."

5.) God Is Sovereign

God's sovereignty is a mainstay of Reformed theology. The
Bible teaches that God is in charge. "Who has spoken and it
came to pass, unless the Lord has commanded it?" (Lam.
3:37) We creatures are subject to our Creator. "Many are the
plans in the mind of a man, but it is the purpose of the Lord
that will stand" (Proverbs 19:21).

No human being engineered the course of history so that
Reformed theological categories would gain increased
acceptance among certain groups of African Americans. But
if Christians understand the causes--both spiritual and
temporal--that lead to the spread of the gospel, we can use
that information to make Christ known among all kinds of
people.

Ultimately, labels like "Reformed" don't matter so much as the good news that Jesus Christ has died for all races, ethnicities, cultures, and classes. So let us make every effort to proclaim this gospel using the means available in our day.

The Old Testament Story†

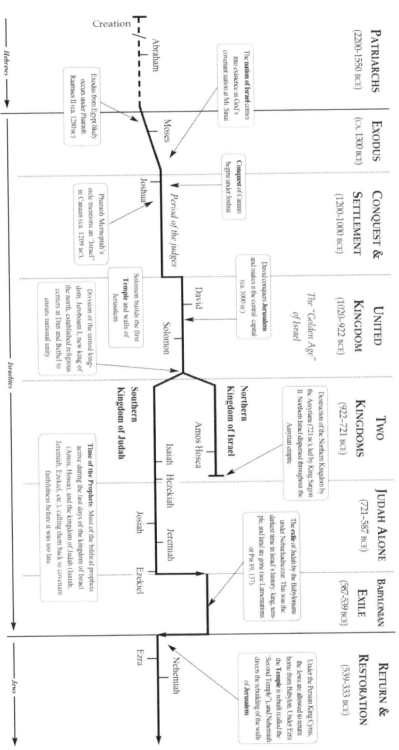

Hebrews

| PATRIARCHS (2200–1550 BCE) | EXODUS (CA. 1300 BCE) | CONQUEST & SETTLEMENT (1200–1000 BCE) | UNITED KINGDOM (1020–922 BCE) | TWO KINGDOMS (922–721 BCE) | JUDAH ALONE (721–587 BCE) | BABYLONIAN EXILE (587–539 BCE) | RETURN & RESTORATION (539–333 BCE) |

Creation

Abraham

The **nation of Israel** comes into existence as God's covenant nation at Mt. Sinai

Exodus from Egypt likely occurs under Pharaoh Ramses II (ca. 1290 BCE)

Moses

Conquest of Canaan begins under Joshua

Pharaoh Merneptah's stele mentions an "Israel" in Canaan (ca. 1209 BCE).

Joshua

Period of the judges

David conquers **Jerusalem** and makes it the central capital (ca. 1000 BCE)

Solomon builds the first **Temple** and walls of Jerusalem

David

The "Golden Age" of Israel

Solomon

Division of the united kingdom. Jeroboam I, new king of the north, established religious centers at Dan and Bethel to ensure national unity.

Southern Kingdom of Judah

Northern Kingdom of Israel

Destruction of the Northern Kingdom by the Assyrians (721 BCE), led by King Sargon II. Northern Israel dispersed throughout the Assyrian empire.

Amos Hosea

Isaiah   Hezekiah

Josiah

Jeremiah

Ezekiel

Time of the Prophets. Most of the biblical prophets active during the last days of the kingdom of Israel (Amos, Hosea), and the kingdom of Judah (Isaiah, Jeremiah, Ezekiel, etc.), calling them back to covenant faithfulness before it was too late.

The **exile** of Judah by the Babylonians under Nebuchadnezzar. This was the darkest time in Israel's history: King, temple, and land are gone (see Lamentations or Pss 89, 137).

Israelites

Ezra

Nehemiah

Under the Persian King Cyrus, the Jews are allowed to return home from Babylon. Under Ezra the **Temple** is rebuilt (called the "Second Temple"), and Nehemiah directs the rebuilding of the walls of **Jerusalem**.

Jews

Cheat Sheet
General Review of the Period

1. Define RENAISSANCE

   Awakening of Europe to a new interest in literature, art and science. The change from medieval to modern aims and methods of thought. Undermined Roman Catholic Church

   1. List 3 major facts about the Bible of the age.

   a. Cost wages of a working man for a year.

   b. Printing led to translation and circulation in all languages of Europe

   c. Reading New Testament showed Papal Church far from New Testament ideal

3. What was the major cause of the Reformation?

   The sale of indulgences by Leo X – his need for money – pardon all sins

4. Explain Who? What? When? Why? Where? For the Reformation.

   Martin Luther – 95 Theses – October 1517 – Preaching against indulgence and striking at the authority of the Pope and Priesthood – Wittenberg Cathedral, Germany

5. What took the place of Councils? Name the two and the cause and effect.

> Diets – Diet of Worms – 1521 – Luther was summoned to the Council of German Rulers to retrace his statements against the Roman Church – Stood like Paul!

6. What two things was Martin Luther immortalized for?

  a. Starting Reformation
  b. Translation of New Testament into German – Foundation of German Language – 1521 – Old Testament not 'til seven years later.

7. Define Protestant.

  a. Those Lutherans who protested against the rule of the princes.

CHRISTIAN OUTREACH

1. Identify the Reformation in Switzerland and how it was different from Germany
   It arose independently in 1517 under Ulrich Zwingli who attacked the "remission of sins". Was organized at Zurich and became more radical than in Germany – Progress hindered by Civil War – Zwingli was slain in 1531.

2. Identify the Following:

Ulrich Zwingli (1520s) – leader of the Reformation in Switzerland

John Calvin (1536) – greatest theologian since Augustine – Institute of Christian Religion – standard of Protestant Doctrine

Jacques Lefevre (1512) – France – Preached doctrine "justification by faith"

John Tyndale (1530) – England – translated New Testament into mother tongue – earliest version in English after invention of printing – martyred in 1536

Queen Mary (1553 – 1558) – Bigoted Romanist – brought subjects back by lighting fires of persecution. Reigned only 5 years. 300 Protestants suffered martyrdom.

Queen Elizabeth (1558 – 1603) – "Elizabethan" – Church of England re-established. It was the most religious age in English history.

John Knox (1505 – 1572) Scotland – Radical leader swept away old religion. Presbyterian Church became established Church of Scotland

3. What unique feature occurred between the beginning of the 16th Century and the end of the Century?

At the beginning – only church in Western Europe – Roman Catholic

At the end of century – every land of Northern Europe – West of Russia – had established its own national church

4. Name and identify the (5) principles of the Reformation.

   a. Scripture – true religion founded upon scriptures – Bible back

   b. Rational – religion should be rational and intelligent

   c. Personal – Pointed worshipper to God – direct object of prayer, giver of pardon & grace

   d. Spiritual – A spiritual and not a formal religion; simplicity and of spirit

   e. National – Protestantism triumphed national church – self governed and independent of Rome

1. What was the Counter Reformation?
   The move to regain lost ground in Europe, subvert Protestant faith and promote Roman Catholic missions in foreign lands. Missionary efforts of Catholic Church one of the force of the Counter Reformation

2. Identify: **The Jesuits** and the role they played.

1534 – Ignatius Loyola – a monastic order – strictest discipline, intense loyalty to church and order; deepest religious devotion. Principal aim to fight Protestant movement – now most potent force for Roman Catholic

3. What was **The thirty Years' War**?

    1618 – 1848. Conflict between Reformed and Catholic' political rivalry as well as religious. In 1648 – Peace of Westphalia fixed boundaries – Catholic & Protestants – End of Reformation.

4. Identify:

    Desiderius Erasmus – Holland; edition of New Testament in Greek with Latin Translation

    John Calvin – France; Institute of Christian Religion – bases of doctrine of all protestant churches except Lutheran.

    Thomas Cranmer – England; First Protestant head of English Church – one of compilers of "Prayer Book"; writer of Article of Religion

    John Knox – Scotland' Absolute ruler in Reformation

    Ignatius of Loyola – (Catholic) – Spaniard; Started Jesuits; canonized as a saint in 1622

St. Francis Xavier – (Catholic) – Spaniard; Founder of foreign missions – India – Ceylon – Japan' died of fever in 1552; only 46; loved by both sides

> *BLACK Facts:* Matthew 1:1-14 contains the genealogy of Jesus in which four Afro-Asiatic women are included; Rahab, Tamar, Ruth, and Bathsheba.

Part 3

The Modern Era Church

Early Modern era

This is the period from the Industrial revolution and the French Revolution until the mid 19th century.

Revivalism (1720–1906)

Revivalism refers to the Calvinist and Wesleyan revival, called the Great Awakening, in North America which saw the development of evangelical Congregationalist, Presbyterian, Baptist, and new Methodist churches.

Great Awakenings

The First Great Awakening was a wave of religious enthusiasm among Protestants in the American colonies *c.* 1730–1740, emphasizing the traditional Reformed virtues of Godly preaching, rudimentary liturgy, and a deep sense of personal guilt and redemption by Christ Jesus. Historian Sydney E. Ahlstrom saw it as part of a "great international Protestant upheaval" that also created Pietism in Germany, the Evangelical Revival, and Methodism in England.[90] It centered on reviving the spirituality of established congregations, and mostly affected Congregational, Presbyterian, Dutch Reformed, German Reformed, Baptist, and Methodist churches, while also spreading within the slave population.

The Second Great Awakening (1800–1830s), unlike the first, focused on the unchurched and sought to instill in them a deep sense of personal salvation as experienced in revival meetings. It also sparked the beginnings of groups such as the Mormons, the Restoration Movement and the Holiness movement. The Third Great Awakening began from 1857 and was most notable for taking the movement throughout the world, especially in English speaking countries. The final group to emerge from the "great awakenings" in North America was Pentecostalism, which had its roots in the Methodist, Wesleyan, and Holiness movements, and began in 1906 on Azusa Street, in Los Angeles. Pentecostalism would later lead to the Charismatic movement.

Restorationism

Restorationism refers to the belief that a purer form of Christianity should be restored using the early church as a model. In many cases, restorationist groups believed that contemporary Christianity, in all its forms, had deviated from the true, original Christianity, which they then attempted to "Reconstruct", often using the Book of Acts as a "guidebook" of sorts. Restorationists do not usually describe themselves as "reforming" a Christian church continuously existing from the time of Jesus, but as *restoring* the Church that they believe was lost at some point. "Restorationism" is often used to describe the Stone-Campbell Restoration Movement.

The term "Restorationist" is also used to describe the Latter-day Saints (LDS or "Mormons") and the Jehovah's Witness Movement. "Mormons" believe that Joseph Smith, Jr. was chosen to restore the original organization established by Jesus, now "in its fullness", rather than to reform the church.

Late Modern era

The history of the Church from the mid 19th century around period of the revolutions of 1848 to today.

Modern Eastern Orthodoxy

Russian Orthodox Church in the Russian Empire

The Russian Orthodox Church held a privileged position in the Russian Empire, expressed in the motto of the late Empire from 1833: Orthodoxy, Autocracy, and Populism. Nevertheless, the Church reform of Peter I in the early 18th century had placed the Orthodox authorities under the control of the Tsar. An official (titled Ober-Procurator) appointed by the Tsar himself ran the committee which governed the Church between 1721 and 1918: the Most Holy Synod.

The Church became involved in the various campaigns of russification, and was accused of involvement in anti-Jewish pogroms. In the case of anti-Semitism and the anti-Jewish pogroms, no evidence is given of the direct participation of the Church, and many Russian Orthodox clerics, including senior hierarchs, openly defended persecuted Jews, at least from the second half of the 19th century. Also, the Church has no official position on Judaism as such.

The Bolsheviks and other Russian revolutionaries saw the Church, like the Tsarist state, as an enemy of the people.

Russian Orthodox Church in the Soviet Union

The Russian Orthodox Church collaborated with the White Army in the Russian Civil War after the October Revolution. This may have further strengthened the

Bolshevik animus against the church. According to Lenin, a communist regime cannot remain neutral on the question of religion but must show itself to be merciless towards it. There was no place for the church in Lenin's classless society.

Before and after the October Revolution of 7 November 1917 (25 October Old Calendar) there was a movement within the Soviet Union to unite all of the people of the world under Communist rule (see Communist International). This included the Eastern European bloc countries as well as the Balkan States. Since some of these Slavic states tied their ethnic heritage to their ethnic churches, both the peoples and their church where targeted by the Soviet. Criticisms of atheism were strictly forbidden and sometimes lead to imprisonment.

The Soviet Union was the first state to have as an ideological objective the elimination of religion. Toward that end, the Communist regime confiscated church property, ridiculed religion, harassed believers, and propagated anti-religious atheistic propaganda in the schools. Actions toward particular religions, however, were determined by State interests, and most organized religions were never outlawed. Some actions against Orthodox priests and believers along with execution included torture being sent to prison camps, labor camps or hospitals. The result of state atheism was to transform the Church into a persecuted and martyred Church.

In the first five years after the Bolshevik revolution, 28 bishops and 1,200 priests were executed. This included people like the Grand Duchess Elizabeth Fyodorovna who was at this point a monastic. Along with her murder was Grand Duke Sergei Mikhailovich Romanov; the Princes Ioann Konstantinovich, Konstantin Konstantinovich, Igor Konstantinovich and Vladimir Pavlovich Paley; Grand Duke Sergei's secretary, Fyodor Remez; and Varvara Yakovleva, a sister from the Grand Duchess Elizabeth's convent. They were herded into the forest, pushed into an abandoned mineshaft and grenades were then hurled into the mineshaft.

Her remains were buried in Jerusalem, in the Church of

Maria Magdalene.

The main target of the anti-religious campaign in the

1920s and 1930s was the Russian Orthodox Church, which

had the largest number of faithful. Nearly its entire clergy,

and many of its believers, were shot or sent to labor camps.

Theological schools were closed, and church publications

were prohibited. In the period between 1927 and 1940, the

number of Orthodox Churches in the Russian Republic fell

from 29,584 to fewer than 500. Between 1917 and 1940,

130,000 Orthodox priests were arrested. Father Pavel

Florensky was one of the New-martyrs of this particular

period.

> **BLACK Facts:** Acts 8:26-40 The Ethiopian Finance Minister on a mission for the Queen of the Ethiopians, the Kandake or Candace; he is baptized as perhaps the first non-Jew (an early tradition that rivals the baptism of Cornelius).

After Nazi Germany's attack on the Soviet Union in

1941, Joseph Stalin revived the Russian Orthodox Church to

intensify patriotic support for the war effort. By 1957 about

22,000 Russian Orthodox churches had become active. But in 1959 Nikita Khrushchev initiated his own campaign against the Russian Orthodox Church and forced the closure of about 12,000 churches. By 1985 fewer than 7,000 churches remained active.

In the Soviet Union, in addition to the methodical closing and destruction of churches, the charitable and social work formerly done by ecclesiastical authorities was taken over by the state. As with all private property, Church owned property was confiscated into public use. The few places of worship left to the Church were legally viewed as state property which the government permitted the church to use. After the advent of state funded universal education, the Church was not permitted to carry on educational, instructional activity for children. For adults, only training for church-related occupations was allowed. Outside of sermons during the celebration of the divine liturgy it could not instruct or evangelize to the faithful or its youth. Catechism classes, religious schools, study groups, Sunday schools and religious publications were all illegal and or banned. This persecution continued, even after the death of Stalin until the dissolution of the Soviet Union in 1991. This caused many religious tracts to be circulated as illegal literature or samizdat. Since the fall of the Soviet Union there have been many New-martyrs added as Saints from the yoke.

Diaspora emigration to the West

One of the most striking developments in modern historical Orthodoxy is the dispersion of Orthodox Christians to the West. Emigration from Greece and the Near East in the last hundred years has created a sizable Orthodox Diaspora in Western Europe, North and South America, and Australia. In addition, the Bolshevik Revolution forced thousands of Russian exiles westward. As a result, Orthodoxy's traditional frontiers have been profoundly modified. Millions of Orthodox are no longer geographically "eastern" since they live permanently in their newly adopted countries in the

West. Nonetheless, they remain Eastern Orthodox in their faith and practice.

Modern trends in Christian theology

Modernism and liberal Christianity

Liberal Christianity, sometimes called liberal theology, is an umbrella term covering diverse, philosophically informed religious movements and moods within late 18th, 19th and 20th-century Christianity. The word "liberal" in liberal Christianity does not refer to a leftist *political* agenda or set of beliefs, but rather to the freedom of dialectic process associated with continental philosophy and other philosophical and religious paradigms developed during the Age of Enlightenment.

Fundamentalism

Fundamentalist Christianity is a movement that arose mainly within British and American Protestantism in the late

19th century and early 20th century in reaction to modernism and certain liberal Protestant groups that denied doctrines considered fundamental to Christianity yet still called themselves "Christian." Thus, fundamentalism sought to re-establish tenets that could not be denied without relinquishing a Christian identity, the "fundamentals": inerrancy of the Bible, Sola Scriptura, the Virgin Birth of Jesus, the doctrine of substitutionary atonement, the bodily Resurrection of Jesus, and the imminent return of Jesus Christ.

Under/During Nazis

The position of Christians affected by Nazism is highly complex. Regarding the matter, historian Derek Holmes wrote, "There is no doubt that the Catholic districts resisted the lure of National Socialism [Nazism] far better than the Protestant ones." Pope Pius XI declared - *Mit brennender Sorge* - that Fascist governments had hidden "pagan intentions" and expressed the irreconcilability of the Catholic position and Totalitarian Fascist State Worship, which placed the nation above God and fundamental human rights and dignity. His declaration that "Spiritually, [Christians] are all Semites" prompted the Nazis to give him the title "Chief Rabbi of the Christian World."

Catholic priests were executed in concentration camps alongside Jews; for example, 2,600 Catholic Priests were imprisoned in Dachau, and 2,000 of them were executed. A further 2,700 Polish priests were executed (a quarter of all Polish priests), and 5,350 Polish nuns were displaced, imprisoned, or executed. Many Catholic laymen and clergy played notable roles in sheltering Jews during the Holocaust, including Pope Pius XII (1876–1958). The head rabbi of Rome became a Catholic in 1945 and, in honor of the actions the Pope undertook to save Jewish lives, he took the name Eugenio (the pope's first name). A former Israeli consul in Italy claimed: "The Catholic Church saved more Jewish lives during the war than all the other churches, religious institutions, and rescue organizations put together."[

The relationship between Nazism and Protestantism, especially the German Lutheran Church, was complex. Though many Protestant church leaders in Germany supported the Nazis' growing anti-Jewish activities, some, such as Dietrich Bonhoeffer (a Lutheran pastor) were strongly opposed to the Nazis. Bonhoeffer was later found guilty in the conspiracy to assassinate Hitler and executed.

Facts: *Acts 13:1 Two of the four prophets and teachers at Antioch (where persons of the Way were first called Christians--11:26) were Africans, namely Lucius of Cyrene and Simeon who was called Niger, a Latinism for "the Black Man."*

Second Vatican Council

On October 11, 1962, Pope John XXIII opened the Second Vatican Council, the 21st ecumenical council of the Catholic Church. The council was "pastoral" in nature, emphasizing and clarifying already defined dogma, revising liturgical practices, and providing guidance for articulating traditional Church teachings in contemporary times. The council is perhaps best known for its instructions that the Mass may be celebrated in the vernacular as well as in Latin.

Ecumenism

Ecumenism broadly refers to movements between Christian groups to establish a degree of unity through dialogue. "*Ecumenism*" is derived from Greek (oikoumene), which means "the inhabited world", but more figuratively something like "universal oneness." The movement can be distinguished into Catholic and Protestant movements, with the latter characterized by a redefined ecclesiology of "denominationalism" (which the Catholic Church, among others, rejects).

Catholic ecumenism

Over the last century, a number of moves have been made to reconcile the schism between the Catholic Church and the Eastern Orthodox churches. Although progress has been made, concerns over papal primacy and the independence of the smaller Orthodox churches has blocked a final resolution of the schism.

On November 30, 1894, Pope Leo XIII published the Apostolic Letter *Orientalium Dignitas* (On the Churches of the East) safeguarding the importance and continuance of the Eastern traditions for the whole Church. On December 7, 1965, a Joint Catholic-Orthodox Declaration of Pope Paul VI and the Ecumenical Patriarch Athenagoras I was issued lifting the mutual excommunications of 1054.

Some of the most difficult questions in relations with the ancient Eastern Churches concern some doctrine (i.e. Filioque, Scholasticism, functional purposes of asceticism, the essence of God, Hesychasm, Fourth Crusade, establishment of the Latin Empire, Uniatism to note but a few) as well as practical matters such as the concrete exercise of the claim to papal primacy and how to ensure that ecclesiastical union would not mean mere absorption of the smaller Churches by the Latin component of the much larger

Catholic Church (the most numerous single religious denomination in the world), and the stifling or abandonment of their own rich theological, liturgical and cultural heritage.

With respect to Catholic relations with Protestant communities, certain commissions were established to foster dialogue and documents have been produced aimed at identifying points of doctrinal unity, such as the Joint Declaration on the Doctrine of Justification produced with the Lutheran World Federation in 1999.

Pentecostal movement

The final Great Awakening (1904 onwards) had its roots in the Holiness movement which had developed in the late 19th century. The Pentecostal revival movement began, out of a passion for more power and a greater outpouring of the Spirit. In 1902, the American evangelists Reuben Archer Torrey and Charles M. Alexander conducted meetings in Melbourne, Australia, resulting in more than 8,000 converts.

News of this revival travelled fast, igniting a passion for prayer and an expectation that God would work in similar ways elsewhere.

Torrey and Alexander were involved in the beginnings of the great Welsh revival (1904) which led Jessie Penn-Lewis to witness the working of Satan during times of revival, and write her book "War on the Saints". In 1906, the modern Pentecostal Movement was born on Azusa Street in Los Angeles.

Another noteworthy development in 20th-century Christianity was the rise of the modern Pentecostal movement. Although its roots predate the year 1900, its actual birth is commonly attributed to the 20th century. Sprung from Methodist and Wesleyan roots, it arose out of the meetings at an urban mission on Azusa Street in Los Angeles. From there it spread around the world, carried by those who experienced what they believed to be miraculous moves of God there. These Pentecost-like manifestations have steadily been in evidence throughout the history of Christianity—such as seen in the two Great Awakenings that started in the United States. However, Azusa Street is widely accepted as the fount of the modern Pentecostal movement. Pentecostalism, which in turn birthed the Charismatic movement within already established denominations, continues to be an important force in western Christianity.

In reaction to these developments, Christian fundamentalism was a movement to reject the radical influences of philosophical humanism, as this was affecting the Christian religion. Especially targeting critical approaches to the interpretation of the Bible, and trying to blockade the inroads made into their churches by atheistic scientific assumptions, the fundamentalists began to appear in various denominations as numerous independent movements of resistance to the drift away from historic Christianity. Over time, the Fundamentalist Evangelical movement has divided into two main wings, with the label Fundamentalist following one branch, while Evangelical has become the preferred banner of the more moderate movement. Although both movements primarily originated in the English-speaking world, the majority of Evangelicals now live elsewhere in the world.

Ecumenism within Protestantism

Ecumenical movements within Protestantism have focused on determining a list of doctrines and practices essential to being Christian and thus extending to all groups which fulfill these basic criteria a (more or less) co-equal status, with perhaps one's own group still retaining a "first among equal" standing. This process involved a redefinition of the idea of "the Church" from traditional theology. This ecclesiology, known as denominationalism, contends that each group (which fulfils the essential criteria of "being Christian") is a sub-group of a greater "Christian Church", itself a purely abstract concept with no direct representation, i.e., no group, or "denomination", claims to be "the Church."

This ecclesiology is at variance with other groups that indeed consider themselves to be "the Church." The "essential criteria" generally consist of belief in the Trinity, belief that Jesus Christ is the only way to have forgiveness and eternal life, and that He died and rose again bodily.

Sidebar

What exactly is the Azusa Street Revival?

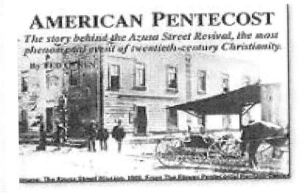

AMERICAN PENTECOST

The story behind the Azusa Street Revival, the most phenomenal event of twentieth-century Christianity.

The Great Earthquake

At almost precisely 5:12 a.m., local time, on April 18, 1906, an earthquake foreshock rudely awakened San Francisco Bay Area residents and it was followed by a massive earthquake about 20 to 25 seconds later, with its epicenter near San Francisco. Violent shockwaves punctuated the strong shaking which lasted some 45 to 60 seconds. The earthquake was felt from southern Oregon to south of Los Angeles and inland as far as 45 miles (70 kilometers) into central Nevada.

It was the most destructive earthquake in North American history. A devastating fire, fed by ruptured gas lines, completed what the earthquake, later estimated as 8.3 on the Richter scale, failed to destroy in its 90 deadly seconds. Some 700 people lay dead among the decimated 514 city blocks.

It was awesome! The unpredictable San Andreas Fault, 800 miles (1287 km) long and passing through the entire State of California, had shifted.

At the time angry men and women, predictably, blamed God. Indeed, within hours a gospel tract was printed and widely circulated in the area, calling the tragedy a judgment and a warning from the God some were cursing.

But that earthquake could have had another cause. In Romans 8:19-21 the apostle Paul declares that *'The creation waits in eager expectation for the sons of God to be revealed. For the creation was subjected to frustration, not by its own choice, but by the will of the one who subjected it, in hope that the creation itself will be liberated from its bondage to decay and brought into the glorious freedom of the children of God.'*

For some time spiritual shock waves had been felt, particularly at two centers, in Topeka, Kansas and Houston, Texas. These early tremors called Christians to pray throughout America and in early April, 1906 a massive spiritual awakening erupted at Azusa Street, Los Angeles. The event was so great that the after-shock waves have been felt throughout the world for almost a century impacting almost every nation of the world. A new Pentecost had come. God had opened up his heavenly portals again and had sent great power to his people once more.

This marked the beginning of the beginning of the Pentecostal Church. Thousands of pastors and leaders from all over the world visited this place of divine visitation, especially during its vibrant early years between 1906 and 1908, and took away the fire of God to kindle the Pentecostal flames in their nations.

It grew very rapidly and has continued to spread like wildfire. There are today over 550 million Pentecostals and Charismatic's who trace their spiritual ancestry back to this awesome event. Currently they are growing at an estimated rate of 50,000 new converts a day! Thank God for the continuing aftershock!

Is it possible that Paul's 'frustrated earth' was somehow aware that *'the glorious freedom of the children of God'* was paramount on God's agenda and that this great outpouring was evidence that the creation itself would soon *'be liberated from its bondage to decay and brought into the glorious freedom of the children of God.'*

The Early Shock Waves

Before the turn of the century many were seeking for more from God, particularly in the holiness groups. Some were offering divine healing prayer with notable results. Others were asking God for a Pentecostal outpouring of holiness and power. From 1901 reports of the baptism in the Holy Spirit accompanied by speaking with other tongues and other supernatural manifestations, associated with the ministry of Charles F. Parham, began to circulate. These early shock waves reflected the spiritual ferment that was increasing in Christian holiness communities.

In Los Angeles, Frank Bartleman, a journalist and holiness preacher corresponded with the main leader of the great Welsh revival, requesting special prayer. One letter from Evan Roberts reports his response: "I pray God to hear your prayer, to keep your faith strong, and to save California." From these letters, Bartleman said he received the gift of faith for the revival to come. And he went on to believe that the prayers from Wales had much to do with God's outpouring in California, later saying that "The present worldwide revival was rocked in the cradle of little Wales?

Bartleman's frequent appeals in newspapers, the Christian press and by his tract distribution, inspired many to seek the Lord. Joseph Smale, pastor of first Baptist Church in Los Angeles, personally visited Wales and spoke with Evan Roberts and on his return helped fan the flames of prayer for Revival even more.

On November 16, 1905, Bartleman, published a statement in a small holiness newspaper called the Way of Faith, which was later seen as truly prophetic. *"Los Angeles seems to be the place and this the time, in the mind of God, for the restoration of the Church."* Little did he realize that this longed for revival was about to break loose amongst the Los Angeles African-American

BLACK Facts: The "mixed multitude that accompanied the Israelites when they left Egypt undoubtedly included various Africans and Asian peoples (Exodus 12:38).

community.

William Seymour arrives in Los Angeles

William Seymour arrived in Los Angeles on February 22nd, 1906 and proceeded to hold meetings at a small store front church Santa Fe Street. This small church plant had resulted from some tent meetings at First and Bonnie Brae Streets held by W. F. Manley's group, the Household of God. The members came from various holiness backgrounds, particularly the Nazarene Church, and were seeking a holiness preacher to be their pastor. Neely Terry, one of these members, recommended Elder William J. Seymour. She had first met this black, one-eyed preacher on a recent visit to relatives in Houston, Texas where Seymour was standing in for the regular pastor, Mrs. Lucy Farrow.

Lucy Farrow was a friend of Seymour's who first told him about the baptism in the Holy Spirit and speaking in tongues. She had received the experience herself through the ministry of Charles Parham, founder of the Apostolic Faith Movement, a growing holiness movement having about 8-10,000 followers in 1906. He was at first interested but had many questions. When Parham moved to Houston and began a Bible School she persuaded Seymour to attend. Because of the countries segregation laws called the 'Jim Crow laws,' Seymour was not allowed to stay overnight in the school. Nor could he even share the same room as white folk. (The words 'Jim Crow' had become a racial slur synonymous with black, colored, Negro in the vocabulary of many whites, or the worse 'Sambo' or 'coon'; and by the end of the century acts of racial discrimination toward blacks were often referred to as Jim Crow laws and practices.) It is generally accepted that Seymour was positioned outside the classroom on the veranda and had to learn 'at a distance.'

Parham had been preaching foundational Pentecostal doctrine (or the 'apostolic faith,' as he called it) for some years and had first-hand experience of Holy Spirit baptism with the sign of tongues. The first occasion was at his Bible School in Topeka, Kansas on January 1st 1901 and in 1903 he was part of an outbreak of revival, which included Pentecostal baptism and divine healing, at Galena, Kansas. Subsequently he began a string of churches, mostly around the suburbs of Houston, Texas, where he also began another college to train missionary evangelists.

It was here at Houston that William J. Seymour, became convinced that Parham's teaching on the baptism of the Holy Spirit, with the initial evidence of tongues, was soundly Biblical and added it to his well established Wesleyan-Holiness theological system.

It was in February 1906 that Seymour received the invitation from Neely Terry to move to Los Angeles and take on the small holiness pastorate. Armed with great Pentecostal doctrine but little personal experience he eagerly set out on this new and exciting adventure. In his own words:

"It was the divine call that brought me from Houston, Texas, to Los Angeles. The Lord put it on the heart of one of the saints in Los Angeles to write me that she felt the Lord would have me come there, and I felt it was the leading of the Lord. The Lord provided the means and I came to take charge of a mission on Santa Fe Street."

Coincidentally, spiritual tremors were beginning to be felt before Seymour arrived. Indeed, it seems the city's entire Christian populace was eagerly awaiting the outpouring of the Spirit, like water coming to the boil.

For his first Sunday morning sermon Seymour boldly preached on the text in Acts 2:4, preaching in no uncertain terms that 'tongues' were the evidence of the true baptism with the Holy Spirit. Without this 'evidence' no one could claim that he or she had been baptized in the Spirit. Unfortunately this was not part of the accepted teachings of the holiness movement, which generally taught that sanctification and the baptism with the Holy Spirit were the same experience, an experience that most of them claimed to have had. Seymour's teaching was taken badly because it challenged one of the most distinctive and cherished doctrines of the holiness church.

The teaching on tongues so upset Sister Julia W. Hutchins, who founded the church, that when Seymour returned for the evening service he found the doors padlocked. Fortunately Seymour had been hosted for lunch at the home of Santa Fe Mission member, Mr. Edward Lee, who took pity on this homeless and penniless preacher and offered him temporary accommodation.

Meetings at Bonnie Brae Street

Seymour spent much time here in private prayer and fasting, becoming known as a man of unusual prayerfulness. Thereafter Seymour invited his host and hostess to share in his prayer times. Much to the consternation of Mrs. Hutchins, other Santa Fe members began to feel a spiritual compulsion to attend these prayer meetings. Lee invited Seymour to minister in a small home Bible study and prayer meeting in the home of Richard and Ruth Asberry at 214, North Bonnie Brac Street. He agreed to this and continued to do until mid-April 1906.

In the beginning, these meetings were attended mainly by "Negro washwomen," and a few of their husbands. Despite the lack of personal experience of the 'baptism' with the 'Bible evidence' of speaking with tongues and the apparent lack of results in his hearers, Seymour ploughed on in faith and assurance that the blessing was on its way.

News of the meetings soon began to spread despite the lack of a breakthrough. Other local church pastors heard about the holiness preacher who was preaching and expecting the next "move of God." Gradually, certainly by late March 1906, these white believers had joined the little group of African-Americans at the house on Bonnie Brae Street and were actively seeking the baptism with the Holy Spirit as evidenced by speaking with other tongues.

It was at this point that Seymour was divinely guided to request ministry from long-standing friend, Lucy Farrow. He obviously felt that she had received the Holy Spirit and was therefore more able to communicate the gift to others. He explained this to the group and money was collected to bring her from Houston.

When she arrived, Seymour announced a ten-day fast to receive the baptism of the Holy Spirit. The entire group fasted and prayed through the weekend. On the evening of Monday, April 9, 1906, before he left for the Asberry home, Seymour stopped to pray with Edward Lee for a healing. Lee, had, earlier, related a vision he had had the night before in which the twelve apostles came to him and explained how to speak in tongues. Lee then asked Seymour to pray with him to receive the baptism with the Holy Spirit. They prayed together, and Lee immediately received and began speaking in other tongues. This was the first occasion of anyone receiving the baptism with the Holy Spirit when Seymour prayed for them.

Rushing to the meeting at the Asberry home, Seymour related what had just happened to brother Lee to the packed meeting. Lee then lifted up his hands and began to speak in other tongues. Spontaneous and passionate prayer for the baptism with the Holy Spirit broke out throughout the house. Soon their prayers were answered when "Seymour and seven others fell to the floor in a religious ecstasy, speaking with other tongues" as they received the Holy Spirit baptism.

Jennie Evans Moore, who would one day become Seymour's wife, began to play beautiful music on an old upright piano, and to sing in what people said was Hebrew. Up until this time she had never played the piano, and although she never took a lesson, she was able to play the instrument for the rest of her life. The phenomenon of tongues and the dynamic message of a personal Pentecost was so exciting that the next night even larger crowds gathered in the street in front of the house to hear Seymour preach from a homemade pulpit on the front porch.

News travelled fast. They could hardly keep what had happened a secret neither did they have any desire to do so. God came in great waves of power and refreshing. The doors and windows were open and "they shouted three days and nights. It was Easter season. The people came from everywhere. By the next morning there was no way of getting near the house. As people came in they would fall under God's power; and the whole city was stirred. They shouted until the foundation of the house gave way, but no one was hurt."

Meetings at the Bonnie Brae house ran twenty-four hours a day for at least three days. People reported falling under the power of God and receiving the baptism with the Holy Spirit with the evidence of tongues while listening to Seymour preach from across the street. Groups from every culture and race began to find their way to 214, Bonnie Brae Street desperately seeking for more of God.

The crowds grew so large it became impossible to get close to the house, and the press of people who tried to get into the house became so great that the foundation collapsed, sending the front porch crashing into the steep front yard. Miraculously, no one was hurt. Within one week it became necessary to find a larger location to house the growing numbers of seekers, hungry for God.

The Apostolic Faith Mission, 312 Azusa Street

A suitable place was soon found and rented at 312, Azusa Street, and the mission was begun. It was an abandoned two-story building located in the old downtown industrial district, which was a part of an African-American ghetto area. Once used as the Stevens African Methodist Episcopal (AME) Church home it had also been employed as a wholesale depot, a warehouse, a lumberyard, a stockyard, a tombstone shop, and had most recently been used as a stable on the ground floor with rooms for rent upstairs.

It was surprisingly small, approximately 60 x 40 feet, flat-roofed and rectangular in design. Outside it was adorned with weathered, whitewashed wooden boards. The Gothic-style window over the front entrance betrayed its former Christian use, but it was generally in bad shape, looking quite derelict. Windows were broken and it was filled with rubbish.

The first secular news reports of the revival appeared, on April 18, 1906 – on the very day of the San Francisco earthquake. The *Los Angeles Daily Times* sent a reporter to an evening service on April 17, and he filed reports that were highly critical of the meetings as well as of the people who attended them. The introductory headlines to the article were 'weird babel of tongues,' 'new sect of fanatics is breaking loose,' 'wild scene last night on Azusa Street,' 'gurgle of wordless talk by a sister,' all carefully calculated to give the appearance of religious mania or madness. (See separate article) Nevertheless, Bartleman reported that this brought the crowds! Many of them were true seekers but there were also the 'crooks and cranks,' even hypnotists and spiritualists came to investigate!

312

Azusa Street

An article published in 'Way of Faith,' October 11, 1906 probably penned by Frank Bartleman gives a friendlier description: "The centre of this work is an old wooden Methodist church, marked for sale, partly burned out, recovered by a flat roof and made into two flats by a floor, It is unplastered, simply whitewashed on the rough boarding. Upstairs is a long room, furnished with chairs and three California redwood planks, laid end to end on backless chairs. This is the Pentecostal "upper room," where sanctified souls seek Pentecostal fullness, and go out speaking in new tongues and calling for the old-time references to new wine." There are smaller rooms where hands are laid on the sick and "they recover" as of old. Below is a room 40 x 60 feet, filled with odds and ends of chairs, benches, and backless seats, where the curious and the eager sit for hours listening to strange sounds and songs and exhortations from the skies, In the centre of the big room is a box on end, covered with cotton, which a junk man would value at about 15 cents. This is the pulpit from which is sounded forth what the leader, Brother Seymour, calls old-time repentance, old-time pardon, old-time sanctification, old-time power over devils and diseases, and the old-time 'Baptism with the Holy Ghost and fire.'

Meetings begin at 10 o'clock every morning and are continued until near midnight. There are three altar services daily. The altar is a plank on two chairs in the centre of the room, and here the Holy Ghost falls on men and women and children in old Pentecostal fashion as soon as they have a clear experience of heart purity. Proud preachers and laymen with great heads, filled and inflated with all kinds of theories and beliefs, have come here from all parts, have humbled themselves and got down, not "in the straw," but "on" the straw matting, and have thrown away their notions, and have wept in conscious emptiness before God and begged to be "endued with power from on high," and every honest believer has received the wonderful incoming of the Holy Spirit to fill and thrill and melt and energize his physical frame and faculties, and the Spirit has witnessed to His presence by using the vocal organs in the speaking forth of a 'new tongue.'"

There were neither hymnbooks nor musical instruments, and no collections were taken. A sign on the wall over a free-will offering box declared, "Settle with the Lord." No teachings or ministries were prepared; everything was left to the spontaneity of the Spirit. The pulpit was composed of two large wooden "shoe boxes." Elder Seymour would usually sit behind these, deep in prayer with his head buried inside the top box. The preaching was simple and direct and covered themes taught in many other holiness missions: salvation by a personal acceptance of Jesus as Savior sanctification by renunciation of sin and turning from worldliness, abandonment of rigid traditions and the legalisms of man-made religion, the baptism of the Holy Spirit with speaking in tongues, divine healing and the premillennial return of Jesus. Often personal testimonies were given or were read from correspondence from those elsewhere.

In Bartleman's 'What really happened at Azusa Street' he states, "Suddenly the Spirit would fall upon the congregation. God himself would give the altar call. Men would fall all over the house, like the slain in battle, or rush for the altar en masse to seek God. The scene often resembled a forest of fallen trees.... Some claim to have seen the (shekinah) glory by night over the building."

"Especially did the enchanting strains of the so-called "Heavenly Choir," or hymns sung under the evident direction of the Holy Spirit both as to words and tune, thrill my whole being. It was not something that could be repeated at will, but supernaturally given for each special occasion and was one of the most indisputable evidences of the presence of the power of God. Perhaps nothing so greatly impressed people as this singing; at once inspiring a holy awe, or a feeling of indescribable wonder, especially if the hearers were in devout attitude."

"Divine love was wonderfully manifest in the meetings. They would not even allow an unkind word said against their opposers or the churches. The message was 'the love of God.' It was a sort of 'first love' of the early church returned. The 'baptism,' as we received it in the beginning, did not allow us to think, speak or hear evil of any man. The Spirit was very sensitive, tender as a dove."

One man at Azusa said, "I would have rather lived six months at that time than fifty years of ordinary life. I have stopped more than once within two blocks of the place and prayed for strength before I dared go on. The presence of the Lord was so real."

Scores of people were seen dropping into a prostrate position in the streets before they ever reached the mission. Then many would get up, speaking in tongues without any influence from the Azusa people. God had come to accomplish His work!

G. H. Lang reports that some who came to investigate were baptized in the Holy Spirit in their lodgings.

"Scores of personal and eyewitness accounts attest that many who came to ridicule the meetings were knocked to the floor where they seemed to wrestle with unseen opponents, sometimes for hours. These people generally arose convicted of sin and seeking God. One foreign-born reporter had been assigned by his paper to record the "circus-like" atmosphere in a comic-relief fashion. He attended a night-time meeting, sitting far in the back. In the midst of the meeting a young woman began to testify about how God had baptized her with the Holy Spirit when she suddenly broke into tongues.

After the meeting the reporter sought her out and asked her where she had learned the language of his native country. She answered that she didn't have any idea what she had said, and that she spoke only English. He then related to her that she had given an entirely accurate account of his sinful life, all in the language of his native tongue." IDFC art.

Other eyewitnesses reported seeing a holy glow emanating from the building that could be seen from streets away. Others reported hearing sounds from the wooden building like explosions that reverberated around the neighborhood. Such phenomena caused onlookers to call the Fire Department out on several occasions when a blaze or explosion was reported at the mission building. The Child Welfare Agency tried to shut down the meetings because there were unsupervised children within and around the building at all hours of the day and night. The Health Department tried to stop the meetings because they said the cramped quarters were unsanitary and a danger to public health. God-hungry Christians flocked in from everywhere.

Bartleman states that "about a dozen saints," met at Azusa on Thursday, Apr. 19, although this may be how many were there when he arrived. Arthur Osterberg, an early member, later claimed the first service at Azusa, was made up of 100 people. The Los Angeles Times reported a "crowd" that included a majority of blacks with "a sprinkling of whites." Weekend crowds were larger than those on weekdays.

Growth was quick and substantial. Most sources indicate the presence of about 300 to 350 worshipers inside the 40-by-60-foot whitewashed, wood-frame structure, with others mingling outside before the end of summer, including seekers, hecklers, and children. At times it may have been double that.

By summer, crowds had reached staggering numbers, often into the thousands. The scene had become an international gathering. One account states that, "Every day trains unloaded numbers of visitors who came from all over the continent. News accounts of the meeting spread over the nation in both the secular and religious press."

Results of the mission's ministry

Needless to say, such phenomena attracted a lot of attention. Hundreds of local believers heard about the baptism of the Holy Spirit with speaking in tongues and went to check it out. The response was mixed. On one hand there was much misunderstanding, disagreement and hostility. Verbal and printed denunciations were common.

On the other hand multitudes had their spiritual thirst quenched by meeting with God. New 'Pentecostal' churches began to appear, most being 'additions' to the denominational churches as Azusa Street was, rather than 'alternatives.' The leaders never encouraged the formation of separate "Pentecostal" denominations. They referred to themselves and their movement as "undenominationalism." They genuinely attempted to remain within their previous affiliations and spread the new Pentecostal theology throughout the churches.

The Azusa Street Mission spawned many local congregations like Elmer Fisher's Upper Room Mission; Bartleman and Pendleton's Eighth and Maple Mission; William Durham's Seventh Street Mission; W. L. Sargent's Florence Avenue Pentecostal Mission; A. G. Osterberg's Full Gospel Assembly; John Perron's Italian Pentecostal Mission; James Alexander's Apostolic Faith Mission on 51st Street (Alexander was one of Seymour's original trustees) as well as one other Apostolic Faith Mission, at Seventh and Sentous; W. F. Manley's Pentecostal Assembly; G. Valenzuella's Spanish Apostolic Faith Mission; William Saxby's Carr Street Pentecostal Mission; and an Apostolic Faith Rescue Mission on First Street.

Further afield, right across America, significant churches became 'Pentecostal' in the following months as visitors came and caught the fire that returned home with them. Seymour and others toured the nation spreading their new-found revelation and experience.

But the most significant growth was seen abroad. Thousands came from around the globe for a fresh touch from the Master. Most were pastors and missionaries. The result of this was a new and passionate host of missionaries, newly baptized in the Holy Spirit, who were dispatched around the world. Both Parham and Seymour were passionate evangelists and the Azusa Street Mission fuelled missionary fires in the hearts multitudes. Soon men and women were now departing for Scandinavia, China, India, Egypt, Ireland, and various other nations. Even Sister Hutchinson, who initially locked Seymour out of her mission, came to Azusa, received the baptism of the Holy Spirit, and left for Africa.

Owen Adams travelled to Canada where he met Robert Semple, Aimee Semple McPherson's first husband. Adams told Semple of the supernatural events at Azusa and of his experience of speaking in tongues. Semple then went with his new bride to China, where Robert Semple would die. But Adam's news had birthed a burning desire in the heart of young Aimee. When she returned to America, she would make Los Angeles her ministry base from where her phenomenal ministry would rise.

John G. Lake visited the Azusa street meetings and wrote of Seymour: "He had the funniest vocabulary. But I want to tell you, there were doctors, lawyers, and professors, listening to the marvellous things coming from his lips. It was not what he said in words, it was what he said from his spirit to my heart that showed me he had more of God in his life than any man I had ever met up to that time. It was God in him that attracted the people."

Cecil Polhill was one of the first Britons to receive the Spirit in Los Angeles and take its message of power and mission back to the UK, where he became a catalyst for the world's first organized Pentecostal missionary organization – The Pentecostal Missionary Union.

The 'Apostolic Faith' Newspaper

In September of 1906 Seymour began a publication entitled, *The Apostolic Faith*. Within a few months, it was sent to over twenty thousand people. Within twelve months it had more than doubled. This publication quickly became the main propaganda organ for the movement. It was filled with testimonies and teachings. Seymour announced his intention to restore "the faith once delivered to the saints" by old-time preaching, camp meetings, revivals, missions, street and prison work.

The influence of the publication was immense and ensured a continuous flow of visitors to the Mission – not to mention the free will offerings that enabled them to advance the work elsewhere. Azusa outreach centers had been planted in Seattle and Portland under the direction of a woman by the name of Florence Crawford.

The irony is that, although the newspaper brought so much blessing and expansion, it also became a major cause of the Mission's demise. Two white women, Clara Lum, the Mission's secretary and Florence Crawford, who was also very active in the work of the Mission, helped publish the Mission's paper, which by 1909 had a circulation in excess of 50,000. But there occurred a serious break between these two ladies and William Seymour. The bone of contention was Seymour's marriage to Jennie Evans Moore.

At the time many viewed marriage as unimportant, even a disgrace in the light of the impeding return of the Lord. One who held these views was Miss Lum, who led a small but influential group at the Mission to denounce their pastor!

Jennie Evans Moore was known for her beauty, musical talents, gentleness and spiritual sensitivity. She was always faithful and loyal to Seymour. It was Jennie who believed the Lord wanted them to marry, and Seymour agreed. So they couple married on May 13, 1908, subsequently moving in to the modest apartment upstairs in the Azusa Mission.

Some say that Clara Lum was secretly in love with Seymour, and left because of her jealousy. Whatever the reason, she relocated to Portland, Oregon, to join the mission founded by Florence Crawford in 1907. The problem was that she took the entire 50,000 national and international names and addresses of the mailing list with her.

This crippled Seymour's worldwide influence. All he was left with was the local Los Angeles list. So when the May, 1908, Apostolic Faith was sent out, though the cover looked the same, but inside was its new address in Portland for contributions and mail. Without realizing all contributors now sent testimonies and finances to Portland without questioning the change. The June issue carried no mention of Seymour and by mid-1908; all references to Los Angeles and Azusa were omitted entirely. Despite a personal visit and pleas by the Seymour's the lists were never returned. It became impossible for Seymour to continue the publication, and this terminated the initial world-wide influence of Azusa and the Mission's worldwide base of support.

Leaders of the Azusa Street Mission, 1907. Seated in front (l-r): Sister Evans, Hiram W. Smith, William Seymour, Clara Lum. Second row, standing (l-r): unidentified woman, Brother Evans (reportedly the first man to receive the baptism in the Holy Spirit at Azusa Street), Jennie Moore (later Mrs. William Seymour), Glenn A. Cook, Florence Crawford, unidentified man, and Sister Prince. Florence Crawford's daughter, Mildred, is seated in the front on Hiram Smith's lap.

The Influence of Azusa Street

The Azusa Street revival had two peaks. The first, initial impact ran continuously from the initial outpouring on

Bonnie Brae Street in 1906, to 1909. By 1909 the explosive power and worldwide attraction began to rapidly decline.

The second peak began in February 1911, when William E. Durham (1873-1912) of Chicago came to the Azusa Street Mission for a preaching mission. This story can be found in the separate article on William Durham.

His powerful preaching, with its emphasis on salvation, the baptism in the Holy Spirit and his new message of sanctification was attended with many of the same manifestations of the Spirit that had accompanied the first great peak of activity at the Azusa Street Mission.

The message he preached had lost the austere and almost legalistic 'holiness' brand of sanctification, bringing with it a welcome freedom and freshness.

At first Durham ministered at Azusa Street but Seymour locked him out of the mission because of his perceived doctrinal error. The crowds went with him, leaving

Seymour and the diminished Azusa Street Mission to struggle on until Seymour's death on September 28, 1922.

It seems a sad end, but, truth be told, its work was done. The good seed had to go into the ground to die, and when it did, thousands of Pentecostal groups sprang into life throughout America and in almost every part of the world. Today millions of Pentecostals and Charismatic's trace their beginnings to Azusa Street and honor the men and women who were bold enough to believe God when they could only see through a glass darkly. Truly they were men and women of faith whose exploits were recorded by God and for whom there will be great reward.

𝕳ighlights of 𝕾eymour's 𝕷ife 𝕷isted by 𝕐ears

1870   Year of Birth Soon After
            Slavery: William Joseph
            Seymour is born surrounded
            by the height of Ku Klux
            Klan violence in Centerville,
            Louisiana, St. Mary Parish,
            amid vast sugar cane fields
            along the Bayou Teche only
            a few miles from where it
            empties into the Gulf of
            Mexico, 90 miles west of
            New Orleans, of Simon
            Seymour and his wife Phillis
            Salabarr Seymour.

1871 – 1894 Years of Growth in
            Louisiana: Seymour
            receives little or no formal
            schooling but works hard,

educated himself in the frontier tradition best illustrated by Abraham Lincoln, drinks in the "invisible institution" of black fold Christianity, learns to love the great Negro spirituals, has visions of God, and becomes an earnest student of unfulfilled scriptural prophecy.

1895-1899   Years of Travel in Indianapolis: Seymour leaves the South for Indianapolis, Indiana, center of the pre-war Underground Railway system for helping fugitive slaves to freedom, finds employment as waiter in a large downtown hotel restaurant near his address at 127 ½ Indiana Avenue, and later 309 Bird Street. He belongs to the (black) Association of Head and Side Waiters, and joins Simpson Chapel Methodist Church, a black congregation in the largely white Methodist Episcopal Church, Northern half of the denomination divided since 1844 over the slavery issue.

1900-1902   Years of New Perspective in Cincinnati: Seymour moves to nearby Cincinnati, Ohio, another former Underground Railway center, where he becomes part of the Holiness movement, influenced by prominent leader Martin Wells Knapp, Methodist evangelist, in whose downtown mission and residential area Bible School blacks are welcome. Seymour joins the <u>evening light saints</u>, founded in 1880 by D.S. Warner, and led nationally by E.E. Byrum, reaching out to blacks in these years. In 1901, <u>saints'</u> leader William G. Schell publishes a book famous especially among black people. "Is the Negro A Beast?" a courageous reply to Charles Carroll's popular racist attack, "The Negro A Beast." Seymour acknowledges the divine call to preach but resists, contracts the often fatal smallpox which robs him of sight in his left eye, accepts this as divine chastening, and agrees to become a preacher, receiving ordination with the <u>saints</u> (later know as Church of God Reformation Movement, Anderson, IN).

1903-1905   <u>Years with Family in Houston:</u> Seymour returns to the South to evangelize and search for relatives lost during slavery. Finding them in Houston, Texas, he settles there.

Winter 1904-1905, he believes divine guidance directs him to Jackson, Mississippi, to visit and consult the foremost American black Christian holiness leader, Elder (later Bishop) C.P. Jones. Seymour always remembers this episode as crucial for his spiritual development.

Summer, 1905, Seymour accepts pastorate of
Rev. Mrs. Lucy Farrow's holiness church
while she is away in Kansas as governess in
the home of Rev. Charles F. Parham. Mrs.
Farrow is niece of Frederick Douglass, famous
black leader. Mrs. Neely Terry returns from
Los Angeles to Houston to visit relatives,
attends Seymour's church and is favorably
impressed with his pastoral manner.

October, 1905, Seymour hears of glossolalia
from his friend, Mrs. Farrow, who returns with
the Parham family to Houston, announcing she
has experienced this phenomenon in the
Parham home.

November, 1905, Seymour leads a preaching
mission in Lake Charles, Louisiana. A young
college student present remembers him 75
years later as 'a very sweet spirited Christian
man, a wonderful preacher.'

December, 1905, Seymour persuades Parham
to enroll him the Bible School just starting, for
which Mrs. Farrow is cook, attending classes
at 9:00 each morning where he is segregated
outside the classroom beside the door carefully
left ajar by Parham. In the afternoon
missionary work Seymour and Parham, preach
together one or more times in the black district

of town. At the public evening services Seymour and other blacks sit in the rear and are not allowed to go to the alter for ministration because Parham practices strict segregation. Seymour clearly understands Parham's doctrine of glossolalia but does not receive the experience.

SPECIAL NOTE: Years 1906 – 1908 are summarized here. See Chapter 3 for further details and footnotes.

1906   Year of Breakthrough in Los Angeles:
January, Seymour travels to Los Angeles, California, where he leads a prayer group to spiritual breakthrough April 9-12. Large crowds including many whites came, requiring a move to early morning to late night continuously. Soon 1,200-1,500 persons are trying to get in the overflowing mission, representing every race, nation, and class on earth. A miracle happens, the color line disappears, and a new type Christian community is born. Word spreads fast across the USA and world, and more people come. Within weeks the first overseas missionaries depart for Scandinavia, India, and China, followed by others to Africa and elsewhere. In September, the Apostolic Faith newspaper is launched with 5,000 copies, followed by steady growth to 50,000 by 1908. Because of the paper, people begin arriving from all over

the world, literally coming from faraway China.

1907   Year of Glory at Azusa Street: As the new year begins the rented mission property, 312 Azusa Street, is bought for $15,000 with $4,000 down. Trustees are appointed, a Constitution is adopted, and the Mission incorporates. The entire year is one of growing influence as other fraternally affiliated missions flourish in Los Angeles, and leaders come from across the USA and world to find spiritual fulfillment, often through humbling their racial pride and notions of white supremacy.

1908   Year of Betrayal Amid Triumph: The years open with encouraging reports pouring in from all over the world. The term "Pentecostal movement" stems from Seymour's usage. He exults, "We are on the verge of the greatest miracle the world has ever seen." Despite an historic financial panic in the USA all the previous year, the remaining $11,000 is paid for the property before April, far ahead of schedule, rendering Azusa Mission debt free.

May 13, Seymour marries Jennie Evans Moore in a quiet ceremony, and a storm of criticism breaks over his head from a small but influential segment of the Mission.

Pentecostalism / Charismatic Movement

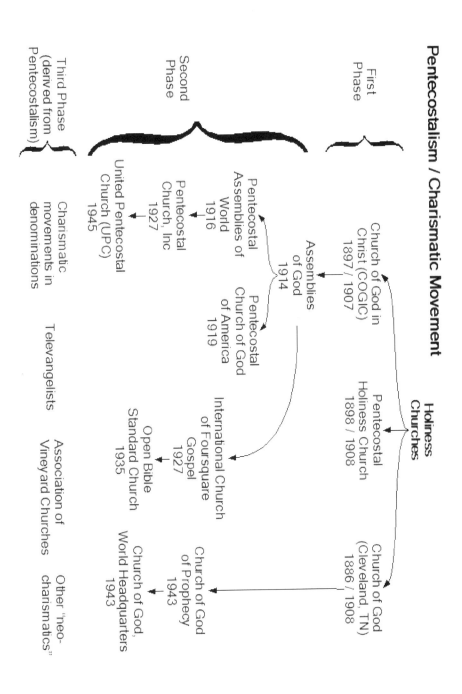

First Phase

Holiness Churches

- Church of God in Christ (COGIC) 1897 / 1907
- Pentecostal Holiness Church 1898 / 1908
- Church of God (Cleveland, TN) 1886 / 1908
- Church of God of Prophecy 1943
- Church of God, World Headquarters 1943

Second Phase

- Assemblies of God 1914
- Pentecostal Assemblies of World 1916
- Pentecostal Church, Inc 1927
- United Pentecostal Church (UPC) 1945
- Pentecostal Church of God of America 1919
- International Church of Foursquare Gospel 1927
- Open Bible Standard Church 1935

Third Phase (derived from Pentecostalism)

- Charismatic movements in denominations
- Televangelists
- Association of Vineyard Churches
- Other "neo-charismatics"

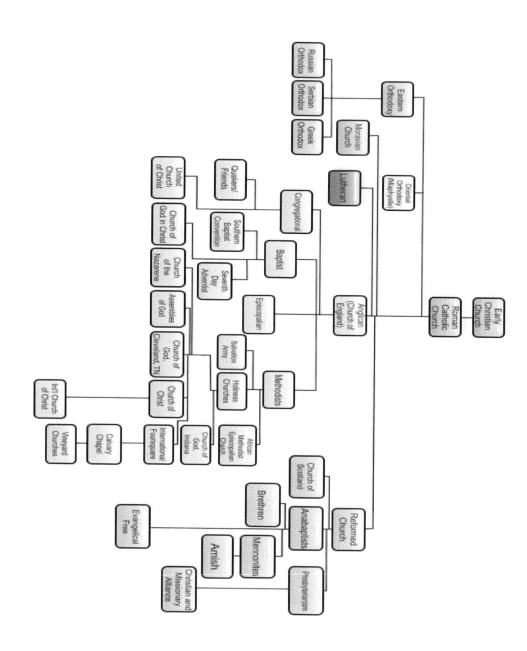

1. According to recent statistics, how many churches are in the U.S.? What is the total membership? How does this compare with the total population?

   265 Religious bodies;

   325,000 churches;

   125,000,000 membership;

   280,000,000 total population

2. Identify the following about the Catholic Church in the U.S.:

When it started:	1494
By Whom:	Christopher Columbus and the Spanish
How souls were saved:	Enslave the natives; enforce their conversion; and compel them to build churches and monasteries
Move To Canada:	Great effort made to win Indians, won friendship of Red Man by kindness and unselfish endeavor
How governed:	Pope – 110 dioceses – 24 archdioceses; 6 cardinal bishops

3. When and where was the first Catholic Bishop consecrated in the U.S.?

   1790 in Maryland

4. Identify the following about the Protestant churches in the U.S.:

   PROTESTANT EPISCOPAL (First one – Where-Role in Revolution-How Governed)

   1st Protestant in America – 1607, Jamestown; 1664 – Dutch; official church in colony; Tories (close to England); 3.5 Million; Bishop, Priest, Deacons, 39 articles of church of England General Meeting Triennially

   CONGREGATIONAL CHURCH (First one-Where-How governed)

   New England, pilgrims, Plymouth 1620, Each church independent – forming own platform – calling and ordaining own minister, managing own affairs.

   REFORMED CHURCH (First one-Where-How governed)

   1628 in New Amsterdam, New Jersey; Dutch Reformed, Christian Reformed, German Reformed, True Reformed, Calvinistic system; local church consistory; form a class – form a synod

   BAPTIST IN U.S. (First one-Where-How governed)

   In 1664 in Rhode Island; Roger Williams, from Anabaptist; a) They believed in baptizing only those that profess faith in Christ (infants should not be baptized); b) only scriptural form of baptism is by immersion of the body in water, not by sprinkling. Each independent, fix own standards, make own rules; no church more united in spirit.

Part 3

The Modern Missionary Movement

It is an assumed thing among the majority of professing Christians today that the theological foundation of the modern missionary movement is of God, and is, therefore, beyond reproach. Indeed, it is considered by the supporters of missionary enterprise well-nigh sacrilegious for any to question the Scripturalness of its theology. Yet, since God's people are commanded to "test the spirits, whether they are of God" (I John 4:1), the theological foundation of missionism can, claim no immunity from this process.

The very history of the origins and theology of the modern missionary movement is little known among Christians today. The name and labors of William Carey might well be familiar enough to many, but all too many are ignorant of another individual, contemporary with Carey, whose views and writings serve as the very foundation of the modern missionary movement. And this individual was Andrew Fuller. It was Andrew Fuller who served as the predominant force, in his person and writings, in the formation of the first modern missionary society, which was officially begun October 2, 1792, and of which Fuller was the first secretary until his death in 1815. An important question which arises at this point concerning these facts is, were the theological views of Andrew Fuller, which served as the foundation of the modern missionary movement, scripturally sound? My answer to this question is an unequivocal no. Indeed, I am convinced that the entire modern missionary machine is founded upon both an erroneous soteriology and a false ecclesiology. I proceed now to demonstrate the facts corroborating these statements.

Shortly before his death Andrew Fuller wrote to Dr. Ryland stating, "I have preached and written much against the abuse of the doctrine of grace; but that doctrine is all my salvation and all my desire" (Works, vol.1, p. 101). In perusing the works of Andrew Fuller, it is to be feared that he never possessed the true gospel to begin with. Indeed, in his desire to deal with the supposed abuse of grace, Fuller did not deal with the so-called abusers, but proceeded to pervert the gospel of Jesus Christ itself. In his works Fuller manifests error in many critical doctrines of the Bible, among, which are total depravity, imputation, substitution, and justification. And it is especially the atoning work of Christ which Fuller tampers with in an artful and subtle manner. And it is particularly Fuller's mutilated doctrine of the atonement which served as both a major impetus to his missionary vision, and as something of a major turning point in Baptist history. And such things have not gone unnoticed among Baptist historians. Let us consider the following examples.

R.G. Torbet notes of Fuller, "To him belongs the credit for doing much to break down the anti-missionary

spirit of hyper-Calvinists" (A History of The Baptists, p. 80).
John Christian adds that "There was another great force
working for the betterment of the Baptist denomination. It
was represented by Andrew Fuller" (A History of the
Baptists, vol.1, and p.350). And Armitage states that Fuller
put a new phase upon Calvinism..." (A History of the
Baptists, vol. 2, p 584). H.C. Vedder writes the following:

The change that gradually came over the particular
Baptists is not, to so great an extent, identified with the
character and labors of a single man. It is still true, however,
that to the influence of Andrew Fuller such change is largely
due, especially the modification of the Baptist theology that
was an indispensable prerequisite to effective preaching of
the gospel... Fuller boldly accepted and advocated a doctrine
of the atonement that, until his day, had always been
stigmatized as rank Arminianism, that the atonement of
Christ, as to its worth and dignity, was sufficient for the sins
of the whole world, and was not an offering for the elect

alone... this modified Calvinism gradually made its way among Baptists until it has become well-nigh the only doctrine known among them (A Short History of the Baptists, pp. 248, 249)

To these quotes I add but two more, the first by Francis Wayland whose following words concerning the extent of the atonement were published in 1857:

Within the last fifty years a change has gradually taken place in the view of a large portion of our brethren ... A change commenced upon the publication of the writings of Andrew Fuller, especially his 'Gospel Worthy of All Acceptation' which, in the northern and eastern States, has become almost universal (Notes On the Principles and Practices of Baptist Churches, p 18).

The second quote comes from David Benedict, whose following words concerning Fuller appeared in print in 1860:

This famous man maintained that the atonement of Christ was general in its nature, but particular in its application, in opposition to our old divines, who hold that Christ died for the elect only (Fifty Years Among the Baptists p 135).

Several important facts emerge from the statements of these historians. First, it is clear that Andrew Fuller did indeed represent a major influence upon Baptists in his person and writings. Secondly, he represented a major influence upon Baptists with his views concerning the atoning work of Christ. Thirdly, Fuller's concept of the atonement was recognized as a significant deviation from what Particular Baptists had previously believed concerning this doctrine. What Fuller advocated is described as "a new phase upon Calvinism," "a change," a "modification of the Baptist theology," and an "opposition to our old divines." Indeed, Fuller's view of the atonement was, according to Vedder, considered "rank Arminianism" by the old Particular

Baptists. Fourthly, Fuller's views of the atonement acted as a leaven among Baptists so that by the late nineteenth century, it becomes "well-nigh the only doctrine known among them." And fifthly, according to Vedder, Fuller's 'modification of the Baptist theology was 'an indispensable prerequisite to effective preaching of the gospel." Here we can see a direct connection made between Fuller's concept of the atonement and his missionary vision. So much then for the testimonies of these historians; it is time to consider the works of Andrew Fuller himself.

In coming to examine the works of Andrew Fuller, the extracts which follow will demonstrate beyond doubt that Fuller did not possess the true gospel of Jesus Christ. Fuller's works are characterized by confusion and subtlety. Indeed, pervading much of his theology is an unfounded and unwarranted paranoia of antinomianism. And it is this fear of antinomianism, I am convinced, what led Fuller to pervert the good news of Jesus Christ. We shall consider first some extracts from Fuller's three sermons on justification. In his first sermon he notes the following:

Yet, to speak of sins as being pardoned before they are repented of, or even committed, is not only to maintain that on which the Scriptures are silent, but to contradict the current language of their testimony. If all our sins, past, present, and to come, were actually forgiven, either when Christ laid down his -life, or even on our first believing, why did David speak of 'confessing his transgression," and of God "forgiving his iniquity?" (Works, vol.1, p. 282).

In these words Fuller manifests several grave errors concerning salvation. First, Fuller's words represent a denial of the finished work of Christ on the cross. In fact, Fuller renders Christ's work on the cross as having accomplished nothing with respect to the forgiveness of the sins of God's people. It is clear that Fuller believes forgiveness of sin does not actually transpire until confession and repentance take place. Such a view denies that any real taking away of sin, or remission, took place when Christ died (cf. Jn. 1:29; Heb. 9:22). Secondly, since Fuller essentially declared forgiveness depends upon the confession and repentance of a sinner, the grace of God is thereby destroyed, and the dogma of salvation by works to set up in its place. Fuller turns confession and repentance into meritorious works which earn forgiveness. His appeal to the words of David are utterly inappropriate and evince he did not understand justification at all. The confessions the children of God make respecting their sins relate to their walk with God, and not to their judicial standing in his sight. The former has reference solely to the sanctifying work of the Spirit, and cannot, therefore, have any reference to the matter of justification.

Further, godly confession and repentance are the fruits of saving grace and not the procuring cause of it. Fuller errs greatly in that he confounds sanctification with justification.

In his third sermon on justification, Fuller states the following:

The acts and deeds of one may affect others, but can in no case, become actually theirs, or be so transferred as to render that justice which would otherwise have been of grace. The imputation of our sins to Christ, and of his righteousness to us, does not consist in a transfer of either the one or the other, except in their effects (Works, vol. 1, p. 290).

To this quote two more concerning the same subject, from two letters written to Dr. Ryland, must be added:

Finally, imputation ought not to be confounded with transfer ...In its figurative sense as applied to justification, it is righteousness itself that is imputed, but its effects only are transferred. So also in respect of sin, sin itself is not the object of imputation; but neither this nor guilt is strictly speaking transferred, for neither of them is a transferable object. As all that is transferred in the imputation of righteousness is its beneficial effects, so all that is transferred in the imputation of is its penal effects... But perhaps, Mr. B. considers "a real and proper imputation of our sins to Christ," by which he seems to mean their being literally transferred to him, as essential to this doctrine; and if so, I acknowledge I do not at present believe it (Works, vol. 2, pp.705, 706).

In these statements Fuller manifests grave errors concerning imputation. The most glaring heresy Fuller manifests is his denial of a literal imputation of both the elects' sin to Christ, and of Christ's righteousness to the elect. The imputation respecting sin and righteousness are in Fuller's thinking merely figurative. He makes it quite clear that neither sin nor righteousness actually becomes the possession of such to whom they are imputed. And yet Fuller, having denied a literal imputation of both sin and righteousness, proceeds to argue that there is a literal imputation (or transfer) of the effects of sin and righteousness! How a literal imputation of an effect can proceed upon a figurative imputation of a cause is beyond explanation. Fuller's sentiments lead inevitably to the conclusion that Christians enter heaven without any

righteousness, and with their sins still intact. Hence,
Christians cannot be said to possess any real justification in
the sight of God. A figurative imputation of sin and
righteousness cannot lead to a literal claim to heaven. Fuller's
view of imputation can only lead to a surreal, shadowy, and
phantasmic atonement wherein Christ's work on the cross is
portrayed as no more than a stage-play, and where no real and
true transaction respecting sin and righteousness can be said
to have been accomplished.

The next statements made by Fuller also come from a
letter written to Dr. Ryland:

Were I asked concerning the gospel, when it is
introduced into a country, for whom was it sent? I should
answer, if I had respect only to the revealed word of God.. It
is sent for men, not as elect, or as non-elect, but as sinners. In
like manner, concerning the death of Christ. If I speak of it
irrespective of the purpose of the Father and the Son as to its
objects as who is to be saved by it, merely referring to what it

is in itself sufficient for, and declared in the gospel to be adapted to, it was for sinners as sinners... (Works, vol. 2, PP-706, 707)

Here Fuller manifests his heretical notions concerning the atonement and its relationship to missionary endeavor. The foundation for Fuller's concept of missionary enterprise is an abstract view of the atonement, one which has no reference to purpose or design. In other words, what we have here is an indefinite atonement. Directly connected to this abstract atonement is Fuller's idea that the gospel is to be preached indiscriminately to all, regardless of election or reprobation. But in both these points Fuller errs greatly. First, Fuller has no Scriptural warrant to speak of the atonement irrespective of a design. Indeed, the atonement of Christ is a design, one which is intended solely for the salvation of the elect. Texts like Matthew 1:21 leave no doubt concerning the purpose of the incarnation, and the design was that Jesus "should save his people from their sins." The sufficiency of the atonement extends no further than its efficiency. The statement "sufficient for all, but efficient for the elect" has no Scriptural foundation.

Secondly, Fuller has no Scriptural warrant stating that God's word declares the gospel is sent unto sinners as sinners, and not as elect or reprobate. It is true that the good news is to be proclaimed unto sinners, but it is not true that this is done regardless of election or reprobation. The fact is, God's word states in no uncertain terms that the preaching of the good news is aimed at elect sinners. In Acts 2.39 Peter declares that the promise of salvation (cf. 2:21) is restricted to "as many as the Lord our God will call to himself." The apostle Paul did not suffer from the illusions of Fuller, for he states in 2 Timothy 2:10 that he endured all he did in his ministry, not for the sake of anyone and everyone, but "for the sake of the elect." And why was the Lord Jesus Christ himself only concerned for such who were "weary and heavy-laden" (cf. Mt 11:28)? Clearly, the reprobate will never be weary and heavy-laden over their sins. These few examples show forth that true gospel preaching is discriminately aimed at the elect, and not simply at sinners as sinners, as Fuller imagines.

We move on next to consider some statements Fuller makes in his magnum opus, The Gospel Worthy of All Acceptation. In this work, Fuller labors to establish that faith is a duty incumbent upon all, whether elect or reprobate. In attempting to prove his point, Fuller establishes the doctrine of salvation by works and virtually denies total depravity. The following examples suffice to prove this.

Faith In Jesus Christ, even that which is accompanied with salvation, is there (N.T.- ed.) constantly held up as the duty of all to whom the gospel is preached ... Though the Gospel, strictly speaking, is not a law, but a message of pure grace; yet virtually requires obedience and such an obedience as includes saving faith... If faith in Christ be the duty of the ungodly, it must of course follow that every sinner, whatever be his character, is completely warranted to trust in the Lord Jesus Christ for the salvation of his soul (Works, vol. 2, pp. 345, 352).

Here again, Fuller is utterly confused concerning the doctrine of salvation. In advocating his main tenet, namely, that faith is a duty to be performed, Fuller is guilty of neonomianism. He rightly notes the gospel is a message of pure grace only to condemn himself in the same breath arguing it requires obedience. How little Fuller seemed to understand that obedience is the fruit of grace and not its cause. He clearly turns faith into a salvation-earning work. Now salvation consists of many parts such as election, justification, regeneration, faith, repentance, and so on. And salvation, from beginning to end, is of God and not man; and it is all of pure grace. Thus, since faith is a part of salvation, and is therefore of pure grace, how then can it be a duty?

Yet Fuller, in making faith the duty of all, detaches faith from the doctrine, of salvation, and consequently, removes it from the realm of grace. Further, in maintaining that every sinner is warranted to trust in Christ, Fuller evinces that every sinner has the ability to exercise saving faith, something the Scriptures declare impossible. Only the elect will ever receive the gift of faith, and thus the reprobate can never exercise what they not only do not possess, but also what God will never give to them. Fuller's sentiments represent a denial of total depravity. Elsewhere in his works, he notes the following concerning total -depravity- "If by total Mr. B. means unable in every respect, I grant I do not think man is, in that sense, totally enable to believe in Christ" (Works, vol. 2, P. 458). Here Fuller flatly denies total depravity, which denial harmonizes with his concept of faith being a duty incumbent upon all.

The words of Fuller speak for themselves. His views concerning such critical doctrines as justification, imputation, the atonement, faith, and total depravity reveal that his soteriology is entirely bereft of Scriptural soundness. Indeed, it can only be described as rank Arminianism. And what is critical for professing Christians to realize is that the soteriological views of Fuller represent the foundation of the modern missionary movement. But this is not all. The very ecclesiological foundation upon which modern missionism began is also erroneous. Fuller, Carey, and others had no Scriptural warrant for forming a Missionary Society. The Scriptures declare that the Lord set up but one institution on earth, namely, his assembly, and that this institution alone has the authority of God to engage in missionary work. Thus, the final conclusion resulting from these solemn facts is that the entire modern missionary machine is founded upon a false theological foundation, which foundation consists of a false gospel carried out by an unscriptural parachurch organization.

What then are the solemn implications of these things? Let the reader consider the following two questions. Can a true convert be the result of the proclamation of a false gospel? Can a true gospel assembly result from the same?

The answer to both these questions is an obvious no. Thus, the only conclusion one can arrive at with respect to what the entire modern missionary movement has accomplished from 1792 until the present day, is that not one true convert, and consequently, not one true gospel assembly, has ever resulted from the efforts of modern missionaries. What then does this mean concerning the countries where modern missionism has performed its work?

It can only mean that there are countries all over the world filled with converts who are not true converts to the true gospel, and consequently, that there are multitudes of churches in the world that are not true gospel churches. Assuredly, a true gospel assembly cannot result from such who are not true converts. A staggering conclusion indeed, but one which cannot be avoided. Andrew Fuller who was so afraid that Baptists would become a "perfect dunghill in society," is to be credited with having produced a missionary vision based upon a false gospel and false ecclesiology, which has since his death filled the world with Baptists who are very respectable in society, but a perfect dunghill in the sight of Almighty God. These words are not written lightly or trivially. A corrupt tree cannot produce good fruit, and thus how can anything good result from Fuller's unscriptural system, to which all modern missionism owes its descent?

Cheat Sheet
General Review of the Period

1. What has Christianity always been? How was this evidenced in the first nine centuries?
   A working missionary institution; First four centuries – church won Roman Empire from heathenism to Christianity – met advancing hordes.

2. What happened to Christianity in the 10th Century?
   Internal fighting for supreme control

3. Give (3) three facts about the **Moravians:**
   Established foreign missions
   Worked amongst Indians, Negroes and Orientals
   No one else had as many missions

4. Identify: **William Carey –**
   Founder of modern missions from England

5. How did the **Baptist Missionary Society** start?
   From a sermon preached by Carey in 1792 –
   Attempt great things/expect greater things

6. How did the **Missionary Enterprise** begin in America?

"Haystack Prayer Meeting" – Williams College, MA in 1811 – Subject of missions

7. Identify: **Judson and Rice –**

Going too far east – changed views regarding baptism – formed the American Baptist Missionary Society and Congregation Church

8. What effect has the missionary work done?

At present – scarcely a land on earth without gospel in one form or another

9. Identify: **Thomas Cartwright –**

Founder of English Puritanism – Church should be Presbyterian and its doctrine of John Calvin

10. Identify: **Jonathan Edwards –**

Foremost in metaphysics and theology in America – Greatest theologian of the 18th century on either side of the Atlantic

11. How did the church view the 2 Word Ward?

World War I – Holy war for God (see page 147)
World War II – church resisted

12. Compare:

Liberals – Bible contains the Word of God

Evangelicals – It is the Word of God

Neo-orthodoxy – Universality of sin and man's need to respond to a holy God – does not address problems of the day.

13. What is **aggiornamento?** Who stressed it?

    Aggiornamento is the updating of the church.

    Pope John XXIII stressed it (1963 – 1965)

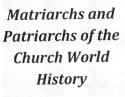

Matriarchs and Patriarchs of the Church World History

.. MARTIN LUTHER

2. RICHARD ALLEN

3. CHARLES FOX PARHAM

4. AGNES OZMAN

5. WILLIAM J. SEYMOUR

6. CHARLES H. MASON

7. GARFIELD HAYWOOD

8. ELIJAH POOLE

9. ROBERT C. LAWSON

10. SMALLWOOD WILLIAMS

11. MARTIN LUTHER KING, JR.

12. MALCOLM LITTLE

13. KATHRYN KULMAN

14. RANDOLPH CARR

15. MONROE R. SAUNDERS, SR.

16. THOMAS D. JAKES

Final Exam

1. What were the Crusades? Why? How many? Results of each one and impact history.

2. Compare and contrast "Islam" and "Christianity"

3. What impact did the REFORMATION have for the church and how did it change the course of history?

4. What was the influence of each of the following on church history: Charles Fox Parham, William Seymour, Charles Mason, and Garfield Haywood.

5. Which ear of church history has had the most influence on your way of thinking and belief? Why?

THE U.S. APOSTOLIC–PENTECOSTAL CHURCHES, 1898 - 2000

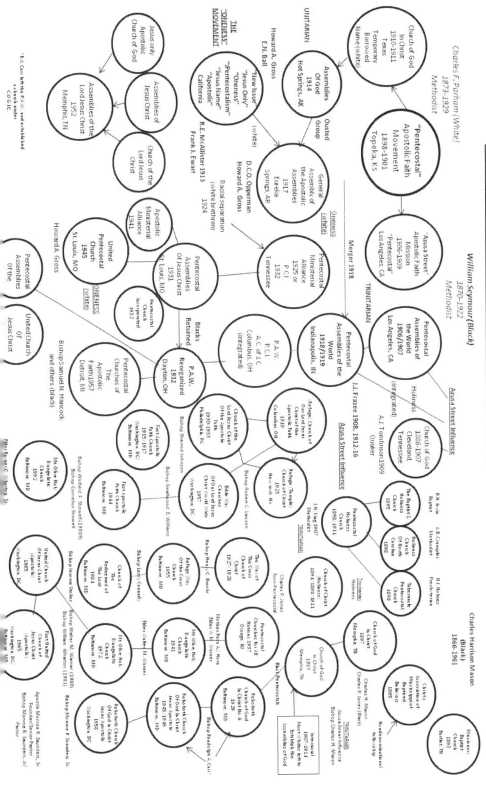

No anthology, historical study, biblical reference lesson, or Christian retrospective would be complete (at least for me) without paying homage not only to the organization I belong to, not just to denomination I may most closely indentify with, not even to the church where I first got saved; I must instead honor the man who made all those things possible in my life and in the life of countless others. The Late Apostle Dr. Monroe Randolph Saunders Sr., was not only the founder of The United Church of Jesus Christ (Apostolic), he was also my father-in-law. I loved him, honored him, and respected him. The following is a brief history of Bishop Saunders and his founding of the United Church of Jesus

Christ (Apostolic) as taken from the official United

Church website. God Bless You.

THE FORMATIVE YEARS

Cradled in the Methodist Church was one destined to become a true Prince of Pentecost. He left his Methodist Church, his family, abrogated his college education, left the place of his birth, Florence, South Carolina, and moved to Baltimore, Maryland. The untimely death of his brother was an extremely heavy burden upon young Monroe, which precipitated the opportunity to father his brother's children. Everyone in his environment noted his fascination, the seriousness with which Monroe took his surrogate role in raising his niece and three nephews. His taking up residence into his sister-in-laws house underscored his commitment to the task of raising those children.

While residing with his sister-in-law, he visited her church and saw and felt something that was totally absent from his Methodist Church experience. He thirsted for the manifestation of what he saw; the church he visited was literally on fire for God. Soon after his visit, he received the baptism of the Holy Ghost and fire. Young Monroe immersed himself in all aspects of church life and activities. The intensity with which he pursued his tasks and the anointing of the Holy Ghost upon his life soon caught the attention of his Pastor. The pastor of the Church of God in Christ #6, Elder Randolph A. Carr, became his mentor as he recognized the deep spirituality of this young man and his creative genius. Pastor Carr provided him with diversified opportunities for church service and leadership. With his dedication, coupled with the training he received in his Methodist background, young Monroe edited and published the church's first newspaper. He directed the church's sanctuary choir; he organized street services; he visited sick members; he held prayer meetings; he taught Sunday School; he directed church dramas; and he taught Bible class. Additionally, he was an anointed preacher of the word.

All of young Monroe's activities showed his readiness for ministry. The people to whom he ministered recognized the call of God upon his life and fortunately his pastor saw, without a shadow of a doubt, the manifestation of the Holy Ghost in him. Bishop R.A. Carr ordained him as a church elder.

Monroe R. Saunders was drafted into the United States Army to serve in World War II. His army experience became a catalyst for his expanded vision of the body of Christ; he experienced a spiritual renewal and deeper understanding of the omnipotence and omniscience of an Almighty God. As an Army Chaplain stationed in Texas, he worshipped in different settings, made many friends, and ministered to large groups of men in the army. The saints in Baltimore undergirded him with prayer, wrote letters of encouragement, and eagerly awaited his return.

Monroe received an honorable discharge from the United States Army. A range of possibilities and options were available to him, but he chose to return to Baltimore. His niece and nephews were now a young lady and young men, but they still relied upon his guidance and fatherly advice.

Young Monroe, now a mature man of 28 years, desired a wife and family. He sought God for a wife and God showed him the lovely Alberta Brockington. He followed the custom of his day, conferred with his pastor and shared the secret of his heart with the hope of getting his advice and approval. He then sought the approval of her father. When God, the pastor, and her father approved, Monroe told Alberta about his spark of love. Although she was 17, she accepted his proposal, and a short and blissful courtship ensued. On July 31, 1947, Monroe and Alberta were joined in holy matrimony. This marriage, which was made in heaven, produced 6 children.

THE SCHOLAR

Monroe's desire to complete the college education he had begun at Virginia State College was still unfulfilled. He did not wish to offend his pastor or others who thought he had enough education, so he discretely enrolled at Howard University, Washington, D.C., as a part-time sociology major. Four years later, he earned his BA degree in Sociology from Howard University, Magna Cum Laude.

Considered by many as a man ahead of his time, he was always on the cutting edge of what many religious traditionalists would deem impossible dreams and accomplishments for Pentecostal Christians. In the late 50's and early 60's, Monroe R. Saunders, Sr. returned to his Alma Mater, Howard University to earn a theology degree. During his matriculation in the School of Divinity, he maintained his high academic and scholarly standards. This Pentecostal minister who had dared to formally advance his education impressed many of his faculty, including Dean Samuel Gandy and Dr. Leon Wright. He successfully completed his course of study and earned a Bachelor of Divinity degree. Monroe R. Saunders, Sr. determined that it was time for him to earn his Doctor of Ministry degree from the Howard University School of Divinity.

In 1979, the educator Monroe R. Saunders founded The Monroe R. Saunders Center for Creative Learning, a primary grade school, which is still in operation.

People throughout the United States, Canada, The United Kingdom, Africa and the isles of the Caribbean respected Bishop Saunders as a scholar, a student of the word, a prolific writer, an intellectual, and an outstanding preacher. He was a man whose intellectual acumen was in submission to the Holy Spirit. This submission produced some of the most anointed, dynamic and inspiring messages known to Pentecost. This was truly a man of spiritual and intellectual excellence.

A PRINCE IN GOD'S CHURCH

In 1948, The Church of God in Christ #6 was re-named Rehoboth Church of God in Christ, Apostolic; it was located from the two hundred block of Mount Street to the corner of Fulton and Riggs Avenues. During this period the pastor said that God had called him to stretch out and had revealed to him baptism in the name of Jesus. The church grew by leaps and bounds. With the new revelation, the congregation received re-baptism in the name of Jesus Christ for the

remission of sins. The pastor, the late Bishop R. A. Carr expanded the local assembly concept into an International Church Organization. Baptism in the name of Jesus and receiving the gift of the Holy Ghost
distinguished this new organization.

Elder Saunders was extraordinarily effective in dealing with hard core cases of resistance to the gospel. Most famous and dreaded were his altar calls. When he fastened his eyes upon the sinner and pointed his finger, declaring "come out of that corner, you cannot
hide," few souls remained in their seats.

The Annual Holy Convocation of Rehoboth Churches Apostolic was a high holy event. Church prelates, parishioners, and friends made Rehoboth Church, relocated to 700 Poplar Grove Street their holy ground for seven days. The time of this grand celebration was 50 days after the biblical event of Pentecost. In 1957, the hallmark of the Holy convocation, was the ordination of Elder Monroe Saunders, Sr. Elder Sydney A. Dunn, and Elder John S. Watson to the office of Bishop. This ordination service was the most anointed, spiritually charged, emotionally moving service that many delegates had ever witnessed. That Friday night the atmosphere filled with excitement and joyful praise as Bishop Carr summoned Elder Saunders, Elder Dunn and Elder Watson to the altar to be consecrated as Bishops. The congregation wept with tears of joy during the ordination ceremony. The three young elders approached the altar slowly; simultaneously they fell prostrate on the floor before God and before the presiding prelate Bishop R. A. Carr. The three young men arose after the consecration with the official title Bishop Monroe Saunders, Sr., Bishop Sydney A. Dunn and Bishop John S. Watson. The brethren received them with thunderous applause, hallelujahs and praises to God.

Bishop Saunders, Sr. and his spiritual father reached a heart rending decision and parted ways in 1965. The separation was painful, and the healing process was long. They loved each other dearly, but because of God's sovereignty and mercy, both men survived the separation and moved forward in The Lord. First United Church of Jesus Christ (Apostolic) was incorporated in November 1965 in Washington, D.C. At that time Bishop Saunders was pastor of the Rehoboth Church, Washington D.C. at what was formerly a Greek Orthodox building at the corner of 8th and L streets. The current Washington Convention Center now occupies the holy spot that holy spot of ground where the church was located. There, at 8th and L the ministry of Bishop Saunders saw the magnetic pull of young college students from Howard University, and other institutions of higher learning. Also, Bishop Saunders was involved with a neighborhood project of revitalization with Rev. Louis Sullivan. The saints from Baltimore journeyed with Bishop Saunders on w weekly basis to 8th and L for should stirring worship services.

In November, 1965, Bishop Saunders, and a small body of praying believers who had been journeying to Washington, D.C. for services, gave their time and finances to purchase the classic stone church building at 3400 Copley Road in Baltimore, Maryland. It became the new home of First United COJC Apostolic, but more importantly, it was a haven for Pentecost. The atmosphere was electrified by the manifestation of Holy Ghost ministry gifts that many saints had not seen in operation. Multitudes visited First United Church to witness this 1965 "Azusa Street . Similar to the Azusa Street Revival in the early part of the twentieth century, there were spectators and doubters; however, many of the casual observers themselves, received the baptism of the Holy Ghost and became faithful members of this "Acts 2:38" church.

Bishop Saunders became an archetype of "a new" Pentecostal ministerial persona. The symbolic relationship between the powers of the Holy Ghost, Bishop Saunders Pentecostal experience, his higher education, produced some of the most powerful spiritual explosion in services he conducted. Bishop Saunders chose to love rather than to condemn, resulting in many souls coming to Christ.

One of the crowning features of Bishop Saunders' ministry at Copley Road was the monthly "Deeper Life Retreat". On the third Saturday of each month, the faithful would gather to be taught some of the most profound spiritual truths by Bishop Saunders.

People left some of those sessions changed forever. Even today one gets goose bumps, and unusual sweating when he or she recalls the experiences of those days. Reports indicated that during those sessions, more than one individual had "out of body experience" into an ethereal realm where only the spirit of transformed man or woman and the spirit of God can exist.

Bishop Monroe Randolph Saunders, Sr., had the undergirding of a group of praying members known as the Prayer Tower.

These intercessors kept the church and the pastor lifted up before the throne of God in daily prayer. Bishop "Monroe" seemed to have been getting younger. With renewed energy, his work load also increased. He seemed ready for new challenges, for new territories to conquer for the Kingdom of God.

By the summer of 1966, ministers and their church congregations from around the United States, England, and the Caribbean entreated Bishop Saunders to expand his vision into an international church organization. Many pastors and preachers wanted to model their church's ministry in the mold of First United Church. Others wanted to affiliate with a Pentecostal ministry that was consistent in word and deed. This led Bishop Saunders, Sr. to establish the United Church of Jesus Christ (Apostolic) He served as the first Presiding Bishop of the new organization.

The church at Copley Road had outgrown its physical plant and a move became urgent. A prime acreage of land was on the real estate market in West Baltimore, for which First United won the contract. In the late 70's the church on Copley Road moved to 5150 Baltimore National Pike, its current location.

In July, 2004, the United Church of Jesus Christ (Apostolic) the organization founded by Bishop Monroe Saunders, Sr., recognizing his enormous contribution to the Pentecostal Movement and his continued work in ministry, consecrated him to Chief Apostle in perpetuity. His influence on Pentecost is etched in the ministries of hundreds of ministers worldwide. They have lit their torches at his eternal flame and they are blazing a trail with his name written all along the way. Many of these ministers are determined to pass on the mantle they received from Bishop Saunders to the new generation of Apostolics. Therefore, this organization continues to serve through churches and ministers throughout the United States, Canada, Jamaica, other Caribbean Islands and Africa.

A GREAT MAN OF GOD

Bishop Saunders, Sr., along with his wife Elect Lady Alberta Brockington Saunders demonstrated their mutual respect for the institution of marriage. Their marriage, of 61 years, is a model and an inspiration to may married people. Additional, over the years, they have counseled many couples and conducted marriage seminars.

Bishop Saunders was a community oriented pastor. To the Baltimore Community, this man was a spiritual giant who maintained the highest level of moral and spiritual integrity. He was a genuine friend who pastored beyond the man made barriers of organized religion. He was a lover of all people; the good and the bad. He mastered loving the sinner while hating and preaching against sin. To the body of Christ, he was an Apostolic Father, one of God's five star generals who rose through the ranks of God's earthly church, with valor and courage, always remaining faithful to his religious persuasion, Pentecostalism. His wisdom, insight and spiritual exploits earned him the respect of ministerial colleagues, and parishioners, in the United States and other parts of the world.

Bishop Saunders was of quiet disposition with a tremendous

sense of humor, but he was also fearless at reprimanding anyone, if the situation warranted it. Reprimand was done in such a way that left people feeling good about themselves, even laughing with joy. It took deeper thinking to understand his reprimand, which was unmistakably there, but couched in the most sophisticated and fun loving style.

THE COMMUNITY'S PASTOR

Bishop Saunders' influence was beyond the ecclesiastical realm. He was a community activist whose activism was not boisterous or flashy but quiet and penetrating. His working relationship with the mayor of Baltimore City William Donald Schaffer was a bridge to help ease the urban plight of the poor, and ostracized and the downtrodden. When the mayor became the governor of Maryland, Bishop Saunders' influence in the Baltimore community was enhanced. He served a 12 year term as a commissioner of the Baltimore City School system. He was the senior citizens' advocate who served on the Maryland State Commission on Aging and retirement Education. He set up satellite ministries on the campuses of many of the colleges and universities in the Baltimore Washington area. With his ministry widespread in the community, Bishop Saunders had the vision of drawing college students – some of the hardest to convert – into Pentecost with a brand of Pentecostalism that was not just pedestrian but scholarly. Bishop Saunders believed in ministering to everyone on his or her level; he also believed in ministering to the whole man, mind, body and spirit.

His influence was not only felt in his immediate community but was interspersed into many countries. In Jamaica, W.I. he started the Voice of Holiness Broadcast that penetrated into every fiber of religious life on the island. People from all ecclesiastical ideologies tuned into RJR – Radio Jamaica and Radiffusion – on Sunday nights at 11:00 p.m. to listen to this educated Pentecostal preacher from Baltimore. This broadcast is still affecting the lives of people today. The Voice of Holiness helped to boost Pentecost from a marginalized denomination of dubious origin to some, into the mainstream of Christian life and thought on the island. Today Pentecost in Jamaica is a respected part of the island's Christian life with a transforming power that reached into the upper echelons of political and social strata.

Finally, we are extremely proud to call him our Father, our Pastor, our Confidant and our Mentor. We shall endeavor to carry the baton he has passed on to us and hand it off to the next generation.

Reference Page

Hurlbut, Jesse	The Story of the Christian Church
Bartleman, Frank	Azusa Street
Cone, James	Black Theology and the Black Church
Dupree, Sherry	Biographical Dictionary of African
Pentecostals, 1880-1990	American, Holiness-
Foster, Fred	Think It Not Strange
Frazier, E. Franklin	The Negro Church in America
Gromacki, Robert	The Modern Tongues Movement

Kuiper, B.K.   The Church in History

Lawson, R.C.   For the Defense of the
                                Gospel

Nelsen, Hart   The Black Church in
America

Roberts, J.D.   Roots of a Black Future

Saunders, Sr., Monroe   20th Century Pentecostal
                                Movement

Sherrill, John   They Speak With
                                Other Tongues

Synan, Vinson   Aspects of Pentecostal/
                                Charismatic Origins

Timey, James   Black Apostles

Tyson, James	Before I Sleep (Biography of Garfield Haywood
Tyson, James Faith	Earnest Contenders for the
Vos, Howard	Introduction to Church History
Wheeler, Kermit	Unfettered Devotion
Williams, Melvin	Community in a Black Pentecostal Church
Woodson, Carter G.	History of the Negro Church
Mellowes, Marilyn	The Black Church
Hingle, Thomas C	Journey of a lifetime
Tisby, Jemar	The Gospel Coalition

Cauchi, Tony

Bogart, Michael

Bibliography: C. M. Robeck Jr., Art. *Azusa Street Revival*, The New International Dictionary of Pentecostal and Charismatic Movements, ed. Stanley M. Burgess, 2002; Robert Owens, *The Azusa Street Revival*, The Century of the Holy Spirit, ed. Vinson Synan, 2001; S. Frodsham, *With Signs Following*,1946.

Summaries Courtesy of The Ultimate Bible Summary Collection

Bible.org

Biblegateway.com

Dr. Robert Everett Johnson, Sr.,

Dr. Johnson is the Overseer and Administrator of the New Jerusalem Praise Tabernacle in the Westport area of Baltimore City where his wife, Elder Jacqueline Faye Saunders-Johnson is the pastor. He is an ordained minister and Bishop in the United Church of Jesus Christ (Apostolic) where the late great Apostle Monroe Saunders, Sr. was the chief prelate and Bishop Monroe R. Saunders Jr. is the presiding Bishop. He is also the church historian of The United Church.

Bishop Johnson was born September 9, 1947, in Washington, D.C. He is the only child born to the late Elder John E. Johnson and Mother Desiree Johnson. He has been married to Pastor Jacqueline Johnson for the past 44 years.

(She is the eldest daughter of Bishop Monroe R. Saunders Sr. and Mother Alberta Saunders). They have three children; Keturah Desiree (Jermaine), Katherine Faye, and Robert Jr. (Leslie) Bishop and Pastor now have five lovely grandchildren - Nicholas, Robert, Amaya, Kamryn and Kennedy.

Bishop Johnson received his high school education in Washington, D.C. He graduated from Eastern Nazarene College in Quincy, Massachusetts in 1969. In 1976, he received his M.S. degree from Morgan State University in Black History. In 2004 he received his M.S. in Administration and Supervision from Johns Hopkins University. In 2009 he received his Doctorate in Religious Education from Outreach Bible College & Seminary in Fayetteville, NC.

Bishop Johnson served in the Baltimore City Public Schools for over 38 years. He also taught at Coppin State University, Anne Arundel and Carroll County Community Colleges. He has been featured in Who's Who in American Education and on the cover of the Afro-American newspaper for his accomplishments.

In the United Church of Jesus Christ (Apostolic), Bishop Johnson is the church historian and teacher. He is a counselor, consultant on Biblical Studies, and conducts seminars and workshops on Church History. He has served in many capacities as a member of the Board of Bishops. He has pastored in Florida, Glen Burnie, MD, and is currently working with his wife at New Jerusalem Praise Tabernacle, in the Westport area, where THE POWER IS IN THE LOVE also currently the diocesan Bishop of the 2nd Episcopal Diocese (New Jersey and Pennsylvania).

Bishop Johnson is an anointed man of God, who preaches and teaches the Word of God without controversy or compromise.

Other Titles Available From Elohim Multimedia LLC

Whose Blood Did Christ Shed?
An In-depth Look at the Bloodline of Jesus and its Effects on the Modern Day Body of Christ
By Briana C. CaBell

Chasing Shadows:
Revelations of a Young Mind
By Briana C. CaBell

Dream Catcher:
Tales of Love and Life, lost and found
By Briana C. CaBell

Meditations From The Minstrel
A 12 Month Devotional
By Pastor Jacqueline Faye Saunders-Johnson

More titles coming soon...